Cindy Petersen

MONEY, MYTHS, AND TAXES

The Wounds of Tax Ignorance

Cindy R. Petersen
PO Box 143
Carmen, ID 83462

ISBN: 978-1-66787-334-3 (softcover)
ISBN: 978-1-66787-335-0 (eBook)

TABLE OF CONTENTS

ACKNOWLEDGMENTS

This book would not have been possible without the support of my amazing husband Terry A. Petersen, my loyal, inquisitive clients, my colleagues, my family, and friends. All who have patiently listened, made valuable suggestions, and encouraged the writing of this book. A special thanks goes out to my children, especially my daughter Caitlin M. Pratt for reviewing the material in this book and making suggestions for editing, simplicity, and format.

I thank God for giving me the benefits of having such a wonderful family, loving supportive parents, wonderful friends, and intelligent colleagues that have made such an impact in my life. I have had many mentors throughout my career along the way that have encouraged me to pursue the goals I set out in my life.

MONEY, MYTHS, AND TAXES
The Wounds of Tax Ignorance

PREFACE

If you believe taxes are supposed to be "fair" to taxpayers, you are sadly mistaken, my friends. There have been many tax laws introduced and passed into law by Congress over the course of the past several years, defining how we calculate our federal tax liability. In recent years, most of those who have become members of Congress became millionaires after they were elected. Have you ever wondered why or how members of Congress have become so wealthy when the salary for serving in Congress runs between $174,000-$223,500?

Tax laws have been written for the purpose of the United States government to collect money via the American taxpayer. Since its inception, federal tax collection revenue has been a main source of funding for the United States government. Throughout history, the United States government has collected many different types of taxes from Americans living in the United States, those living abroad, as well as foreign nationals earning money from United States sources. The Internal Revenue Service (IRS) is the agency responsible for collecting money from taxpayers for Congress to distribute as it sees fit. Congress holds the purse of the United States.

The IRS is responsible for collecting taxes, ensuring compliance by taxpayers, and administering the Internal Revenue Code (IRC). The IRS is part of the Department of the Treasury and is led by the Commissioner of Internal Revenue, appointed to a five-year term by the President of the United States. The duties of the IRS include providing tax assistance to taxpayers, pursuing and resolving instances of erroneous or fraudulent tax filings, and overseeing general tax code practices and procedures.

The Sixteenth Amendment to the Constitution gives the right to the United States Government to collect taxes from both Americans and some foreign individuals and is the law of this land. Over the years taxpayers have had a very negative view of the IRS. The IRS is after all, the collection agency for the United States government. This is not to say that a great deal of their bad reputation is undeserved. And through the years the IRS has been involved in unscrupulous behavior. But when was the last time you heard of a collection's agent being understanding and sympathetic to the debtor's situation?

Understanding the United States tax system and its history is the key to developing strategic successful tax planning for the average taxpayer. This knowledge assists in formatting the right conversations you should have with tax professionals and congressional representatives.

HISTORY OF FEDERAL INCOME TAX

The United States tax system is complicated and frustrating to most taxpayers. The evolution of the tax system in the United States is even more astounding. That is why it is important to have knowledge in income tax history so you, as the taxpayer, can begin to ask the right questions when paying your federal taxes.

While taxpayers ask why their tax bill is so much every year, not enough consider some of the most important questions, like where do all the taxes collected from me go? How do my tax dollars benefit me? Are the taxes I pay wasted on things that do not benefit me, my family's future, or our country's future?

I once saw a billboard that read that a fine is a penalty for doing wrong and a tax is a fine for doing well. However, most taxpayers understand that the United States could not function as a country without some type of tax collection from its citizens. But a vast majority of taxpayers believe the United States taxation system is unfair or unbalanced. It is important to recognize that the United States government does not generate its own income. United States taxpayers are a revenue-generating source that enables the government to function.

Let us dive into the history of how the federal taxing system first began and how our taxation system has supported the United States over the years.

American Revolutionary War

The dilemma of financing of the Revolutionary War against Great Britain was the beginning of the historical need for funds from the American colonists. With this critical need of financing the American Revolutionary

War, appointed delegates of the newly formed government issued hand signed paper money in the form of bills of credit known as Continental Dollars. These bills of credit were the governments promise to the American colonists that they would recover their money in coins. The American colonists had faith they would recover the money demanded of them by Congress to contribute to the funding of the American Revolutionary War. American colonists complied, with most even believing it was their patriotic duty to contribute.

With growing colonial debt, and to ensure proper accounting, in April 1776 Congress established the Treasury Office of Accounts. This office was responsible for settlement of public accounts. The Treasury was to report the claims for coin and the progress to Congress.

After the signing of the Declaration of Independence on July 4, 1776, the newly formed nation was able to secure loans from other countries to help finance the War of Independence. This would be just the beginning of the United States' national debt. To form an organized financial administration, the first Treasury of the United States was established in May 1777.

Despite all efforts by Congress, and even with the infusion of loans obtained domestically and from other countries, the value of the Continental Dollar declined rapidly and was bearing a return of as little as $1 to every $1,000. As you can understand, Americans were angered over the worthless money. Colonists formed large protests throughout the colonies. The effect of this was the formation of the office of the Superintendent of Finance in 1781. This office was intended to restore the nation's financial stability and to pay the debt to the colonists as well as to the foreign countries the Unites States had borrowed money from, and to make the United States more financially secure.

The official Department of Treasury was established by Congress in 1789. Alexander Hamilton was named the first Secretary of Treasury. He was assigned the duty of submitting reports to Congress on the progress of financial stability and repayment of the debts of the country. The Department of Treasury would become a permanent institution for management of government finances. It was established in part, as a response to the turmoil of the American Revolutionary War and the financial anguish of the United States.

At the time of its creation, Congress had no authority at this time to levy or collect taxes on individuals. The Department of Treasury was originated to collect sales taxes from those involved in distilling spirits (whiskey mostly), tobacco, sugar, property sales and slavery sales for the newly formed United States. In addition to collecting taxes to pay United States government debts, the taxes would be used to build a defense for the United States as well.

War of 1812

With James Madison as President, the United States declared war on Great Britain. This would become known as the War of 1812. To fund the war, the nation's first sales tax on minerals was established. Great Britain retaliated against the United States on August 24th, 1814, because of the burning of York in 1813, by entering the United States and setting fire to the Capitol and the Treasury building, which was completely burned down.

Congress temporarily reversed their position of sales taxes on minerals, distilled spirits, tobacco, sugar, and all internal taxes after the Treasury building was destroyed. Congress abolished the department of the Secretary of Treasury and terminated the Treasury's authority to collect these taxes. With no government headquarters, Congress had lost the organizational foundation for the Department of Treasury.

In the year of 1793, Congress allocated money to start re-construction and completion of the United States Capitol Building. Only the Capitol's east and south wing had been completed by 1814, when the British soldiers burned it down.

Rebuilding and completion of the Capitol Building started back up in 1815 and lasted until 1829. Up to this point, the United States had spent $2.4 million dollars on construction and reconstruction of the Capitol Building, adding to the United States debt.

But Congress was not done spending money on the Capitol Building, Additional chambers, office buildings and the cast-iron dome would be added. By the time of its completion in 1867, the United States had spent approximately $8.1 million dollars on the Capitol Building.

The Treasury building was rebuilt in 1836, under the leadership of President Andrew Jackson. Once again, the sales taxes on minerals, distilled spirits, tobacco, and the sugar tax collection resumed.

American Civil War (1861–1865)

In 1862 President Abraham Lincoln signed a revenue tax measure into law to pay for expenses related to the American Civil War. This measure would be the nation's first income tax and would facilitate the creation of a Commissioner of Internal Revenue.

This person would lay the foundation for the nation's first income tax on individuals. This would also be the beginning of the first progressive tax on United States citizens, even though Congress did not yet have constitutional authority to tax individuals based on income.

The original United States Constitution, prior to amendments, called for *"direct taxes to be apportioned amount the several states according to their respective Numbers."* This meant direct taxes were to be calculated based on the population of each state, not based on an individual's income.

This revenue tax measure called for persons earning from $600 to $10,000 per year to pay a 3 percent tax on their income. Those earning over $10,000 were to pay a 5 percent tax on income. To put this in perspective, $600 in 1862 would be the equivalent of $17,603 today. The United States was still a relatively new country and quite a few Americans paying 3 percent in taxes were by today's standards were not wealthy people by any means.

The Revenue Act of 1862 also included provisions for a heavy tax on alcohol and tobacco. This federal income tax measure was intended to be temporary. The United States government needed the money to pay for expenses of rebuilding the country and building the railroad after the Civil War. The individual income tax provision was set to expire a decade later. But the government had become accustomed to having these funds to spend, so the individual income tax provision became a mainstay of funding for the United States government.

The Revenue Act of 1862 included provisions that prompted more aggressive tax authority. Under the Revenue Act, the Commissioner of the Internal Revenue was again given the power to collect taxes and enforce collection through seizures of property and income, as well as prosecution of tax evaders. Failure to report and pay the appropriate amount of tax resulted in a penalty equal to 100 percent of the tax.

Income tax rates were increased in 1864 so that people making between $600 to $5,000 were taxed at 5 percent, and people making more than $5,000 were paying 10 percent. An income of $5,000 during 1864 was the approximate equivalent value of $94,367 by today's standards and there was no such thing as a standard deduction. Income tax was calculated on gross incomes of individuals. During this period, the inflation rate was an astounding 24.6 percent.

With heavy public hostility to the personal income tax, prompted by tax rates increasing and inflation swallowing most of Americans income,

Congress cut the tax rate in 1867 to 5 percent for everyone making over $5,000. Those making below $5,000 were no longer required to pay individual income taxes. To offset the loss of individual income tax collection, Congress once again began aggressively collecting over 90 percent of the government's revenue from taxing alcohol and tobacco. In 1872, the Income Tax Act was repealed entirely under the leadership of President Ulysses S. Grant.

A decade later, the Pension Act was signed into law July 14, 1882, by President Chester A. Arthur. The Pension Act was fundamentally a type of social security but only for disabled veterans of the Civil War, those still alive who were disabled from the Revolutionary War, orphans, and widows of both wars. The Pension Act was primarily funded by sales tax collection. To be eligible to collect pension funds, recipients had to prove that their disability or death was directly linked to military service. However, the eligibility approval process was very rigid as it required confirmation by both the Adjutant General's Office and the Navy Department. This resulted in few applications being granted.

Post-Civil War

The United States suffered what became known as the Long Depression after the Civil War, starting in 1873 and lasting until 1879. The onset of this for the United States was due to railroad expansion funding. Some of America's largest banks funded the railroad expansion using investors' money. The investors who invested money did not understand complexity of these financial projects. When railroad companies financially failed, the large banks backing them failed as well. This led to the stock market crashing, which led to Panic of 1873. Approximately 18,000 businesses, including hundreds of banks, and some states in the United States went bankrupt at the same time.

Along with the Panic of 1873 after the war, individual property claims by numerous United States citizens who were claiming losses against the United States government started flooding the Treasury Department. United States citizens were claiming losses for property taken during the Civil War.

Most of the claims were for horses and other personal property taken to support Civil War efforts. The American citizens were in financial panic. Numerous people began to look to the United States government to make them whole again. The losses people were claiming were not limited to horses, though. People were claiming their metal pots were sterling silver pots, logs used for building log cabins were milled black walnut, and rowboats were claimed to be the equivalent of yachts.

Once the volume of these loss claims started growing, it did not take the United States Government long to realize that there were more claims for horse losses than actual horses lost during the Civil War. The federal government attained knowledge that it was not the people who suffered the losses making their own property claims. The loss claims against the United States government were coming from agents hired by individuals who lost the property. At the time, CPAs did not exist yet, ethical requirements for attorneys were very relaxed, and people had very few other options for representation against the government. The United States government also learned that these agents were actively seeking people out who may have a loss claim against the government. These agents were offering to collect on citizen's claims for a percentage of what they could collect.

President Chester A. Author responded to these property loss claims by signing into law the Horse Act of 1884. This law was intended to fight against fraudulent post-war loss claims. The Horse Act created a standard for representatives who could represent citizens against the United States government. The standard included suitability checks, background checks, criminal record checks, proof of moral character, and testing for knowledge. People who passed these requirements were designated as an Enrolled Agent. Enrolled Agents remain the only federally licensed tax professionals allowed to represent individuals and businesses against the United States Treasury Department to this day.

Income Tax Revived

The Treasury Department again received a name change. The Bureau of Internal Revenue was renamed in 1894, with President Grover Cleveland signing the Wilson Tariff Act into law. This law included a revived version of the personal income tax on individuals and businesses, even though Congress still did not have constitutional authority to collected income taxes on individuals based on income earned. Once again, Congress looked at the United States citizens to ease the government's financial shortfalls.

During his Presidency, President Cleveland also was known to veto many Civil War veterans' private pension bills put before him, because he believed most of the claims were fraudulent. And even though the pension was restricted by the degree of the veteran's disability, he sternly believed most to be unfounded. President Cleveland also vetoed pension bills for dependents of disabled veterans.

The Wilson-Gorman Tariff bill became law in 1894, even though President Cleveland would not sign or veto it. The Wilson-Gorman bill again reiterated personal income taxes on individuals based on income earned. The tax was a 2 percent income tax on all personal income over $4,000 and on all corporate income above operating expenses. Personal income of $4,000 would be the equivalent of approximately $137,820 today. The 2 percent tax was on incomes in their entirety, meaning there were no standard deductions, no personal exemptions, etc. allowed to reduce the income before tax was to be calculated.

Income Tax Declared Unconstitutional

In 1895 the Supreme Court declared the Income Tax of 1894 unconstitutional in a major court case, *Pollock v. Farmers' Loan & Trust Co.* It was declared unconstitutional because it was a direct tax that had not been properly apportioned among the states by population, which was how the constitution was written. The United States Constitution was a major factor in the way the colonies, not the colonists, were demanded to pay taxes to help fund the Revolutionary War from the beginning.

After the Supreme Court declared an income tax to be unconstitutional, Congress created a joint resolution requiring income tax returns be destroyed. But Congress could not tame their appetite for government spending projects. The government had become accustomed to having taxpayer funds to subsidize the government and sales tax just was not enough.

Sixteenth Amendment to the U.S. Constitution Signed into Law

President William Howard Taft proposed to Congress in 1909 a constitutional amendment that would give Congress the power to lay, collect, and levy income taxes on individuals and corporations without apportioning the burden among states by population. Congress passed this legislation and President Taft signed it into law. The bill signed into law also included a 1 percent corporate tax imposed on net corporate incomes more than $5,000 that year.

On July 2nd, 1909, Congress passed the Sixteenth Amendment to the U.S. Constitution. The ratification of this amendment to the constitution took place under President William Howard Taft on February 3rd, 1913, but took full force when President Woodrow Wilson took office on March 4th, 1913.

The Sixteenth Amendment granted Congress the power to constitutionally impose a tax on individual and corporate sources of income. It gave

Congress the power to impose and collect taxes on all sources of income, regardless of the source the income derived, without the necessity of apportioning taxes among the several states, and without requiring apportionment to be determined by any census or enumeration.

Soon after the passage of the Sixteenth Amendment, Congress passed a 1 percent tax on net personal income exceeding $3,000 or more per year. Although the Sixteenth Amendment increased the number of Americans subject to personal income tax, it was still a tax on people making a substantial amount of money by today's standards. The common American households' earnings were not subject to individual income taxation yet.

The American population was approximately 97 million people at the time. Yet only approximately 188,866 tax returns filed in 1913 were subject to the new 1 percent income tax. The Sixteenth Amendment included a 6 percent surtax on incomes of more than $500,000. Congress repealed the 1 percent corporate income tax. The newly renamed Bureau of Internal Revenue was given the authority by Congress to assess, collect, and enforce tax laws once again.

The Sixteenth Amendment included language that would allow for a personal exemption of $3,000 for single individuals and $4,000 for married couples to be deducted before calculating the tax amount. It also included language that allowed for itemized deductions for things such as state and local taxes and all forms of interest.

The ratification process of the Sixteenth Amendment was not welcomed by all of the States. Of the 48 states, 12 would initially reject the amendment. Some of the hold-out states that rejected the Sixteenth Amendment included Connecticut, Rhode Island, and Utah. Other states like Pennsylvania, Virginia, and Florida did not want to participate in this ratification process at all.

When the first income tax laws became effective, the Enrolled Agent's role expanded to include claims for monetary relief for citizens who firmly believed the new tax structure had become inequitable for income earners in the upper-middle class. But the Sixteenth Amendment included language that would open the door for the income tax structure to expand, including higher tax rates and a greater number of Americans subject to the tax. The citizens who feared the language and called on Congress for greater representation would be proven right over time.

Post Sixteenth Amendment

President Woodrow Wilson signed into law the new legislation that lowed tariffs and at the same time included graduated federal income tax rates. By December 1913, President Wilson had signed into law the Federal Reserve Act. The lowest income tax rate at the time was 1 percent for taxpayers earning between zero and $20,000 after allowing for the taxpayer's personal exemption amount. The top income tax rate for taxpayers earning over $500,000 was 7 percent.

The tax rate of 1913 remained the same until it increased 1916. Not only did the tax rate increase to 2 percent on income earners up to $20,000, but the progressive income tax brackets also changed. Taxpayers earning between $100,000 and $150,000 were now at the 7 percent tax rate and the top income tax rate increased to 15 percent for high earning taxpayers. The individual income tax rates still targeted the top earners in the United States.

The Child Labor Law and the law limiting railroad workers to eight-hour days were also signed into law by President Woodrow Wilson in 1916. The Child Labor Law set a standard for the age at which children could participate in employment activities.

United States Enters WWI

After President Wilson won re-election, in April 1917 President Wilson declared that we could no longer stay out of WWI. He asked Congress for a declaration of war on Germany. Once again, progressive federal income taxation was needed for war funding.

During 1917, the top tax rates for income earners over $2 million was 67 percent. The lowest tax rate of 2 percent remained the same in 1917, but the amount of taxable money a taxpayer could earn was drastically reduced. Taxpayers earning taxable income of even $2,000 were subject to the 2 percent tax rate after factoring in their personal exemption amounts of $3,000 for single individuals and $4,000 for married couples. This would mean people earning approximately $46,300 by today's standards were now subject to 2 percent income tax rates. This would subject approximately 1.8 million United States citizens to income tax filing requirements. The average individual taxable income in 1917 was between $1,500 and $5,500 per year, with over 33,000 households paying from between 2 percent to 5 percent in income taxes. Charitable deductions were also now allowed as an itemized deduction offsetting tax liability.

Income taxes funded one-third of the cost of World War I, with the remaining war funding coming from other sources such as the sale of government bonds. World War I would ultimately cost the United States approximately $32 billion. This would be the Federal Reserve's first major test. Congress debated raising the income rates to create more equity in the funding of the war. Roughly 22 percent of the nation's wealthiest taxpayers were paying approximately 96 percent of the income taxes in the United States.

The Revenue Act of 1918 was signed into law by President Woodrow Wilson on February 24, 1919. It codified all existing tax laws, raised even more taxes, and imposed a progressive income tax structure with rates between 6 percent for the lowest tax brackets earning $4,000 or more, to as high as 77 percent for income earners above $1 million. In 1919, $4,000 was the equivalent of earning approximately $68,500 today. Approximately only 5 percent of the population paid federal income tax at this time, which was an increase of approximately 1 percent paying federal income tax in 1917.

Post WWI

The Prohibition on the sale, manufacturing, or transport of intoxicating beverages was signed into law by President Woodrow Wilson. This law would be the Eighteenth Amendment to the Constitution, which was ratified on January 16, 1919.

Prohibition would be in full force by January of 1920 and the Commissioner of the Internal Revenue was initially given the responsible to enforce Prohibition. This made sense at the time, as the Internal Revenue had been historically responsible for collecting taxes on alcohol beverage sales. The enforcement duties would be transferred to the Department of Justice eleven years later.

In an answer to losing the revenue from "sin" taxes on alcohol, Congress once again raised the income rates to 6 percent for taxpayers earning up to $4,000 in taxable income, and up to 77 percent for the top income earners. The progressive tax rates become more aggressive as well. Tax rates jumped to 12 percent for those earning $4,000 to $5,000.

Organized crime rose in the United States during Prohibition. The Internal Revenue realized that liquor enforcement was virtually ineffective in most cities across the United States because the crime syndicates were running most of the illegal liquor sales. The United States Treasury launched creative means of prosecution through tax evasion enforcement. The concept was to target crime organizations by following the money. Tax evasion is what led to the successful conviction of the infamous mob boss Al Capone.

This was meant to be message to the crime bosses throughout the United States.

The approach had little effect due to organized crime groups supplying Americans with alcohol. In 1933 the Eighteenth Amendment was repealed, and the IRS was once again given the responsibility to collect and enforce tax on alcohol sales and for administering the National Firearms Act.

The Great Depression

Between WWI and WWII America suffered the Great Depression. The Great Depression started in 1929, and lasted until 1941. But even the Great Depression and the financial pain of American citizens did not curb government building and spending projects in Washington DC after WWI. Significant spending had become commonplace for Congress. One very costly project, in 1929, was for the construction of the new Internal Revenue Building. The completed project was at a cost of $6 million to the American taxpayer. Today, that would be the equivalent of approximately $104 million.

That was not the only expensive building project Congress allocated money for. The United States Supreme Court Building started construction in 1929 and would ultimately cost the American taxpayers $9.4 million. That is the approximate equivalent of over $203 million today. Construction on the United States Supreme Court would not be completed until 1935.

Herbert Hoover was president at the time and federal individual income tax rates were as high as 25 percent on the top income earnings all while United States citizens were in deep financial despair. Americans were standing in bread lines, but Congress could not control their appetite for spending. As frustrating as it may be for many Americans, spending taxpayers' money on excessive government projects had become second nature for Congress.

In addition to the new Internal Revenue Building, government building expenditures during the years of the Great Depression included the US Agriculture South Building in Washington D.C. The building on this project began construction in 1930 and lasted until 1936. Congress had excused the excessive spending, claiming it was providing badly needed employment for the American people. Although it did provide employment to a lot of Americans, it did not soften the blow for the millions of Americans struggling to provide for their families.

Social Security Tax Implementation

Before the Social Security Act of 1935, widows, disabled veterans, and orphans of the Civil War could apply for a government pension that was only allotted to veterans with disabilities directly linked to military service. There were no programs available for aging Americans unless you were a veteran disabled in war or a widowed spouse or child of a deceased person with the death directly linked to war.

During the Great Depression, most ageing Americans had no form of retirement income. A means for older men to have the opportunity to retire and still have financial support was recognized by President Franklin D. Roosevelt and supporters of the Social Security Act of 1935. He signed a limited form of a Social Security Program into law by on August 14, 1935. The Social Security Act was implemented as a means of social insurance to help impoverished senior citizen, widows, and fatherless children. This was also the beginning of government-issued Social Security numbers. There were exclusions from the early social security program. People who were self-employed, field hands, and domestic workers were excluded from the new social security program.

The Social Security Act was funded by taxing wage earners paying 1 percent on their first $3,000 of income and taxing employers 1 percent matching funds on their employees' first $3,000 of wages. There were no exemptions allowed before the tax calculation.

There was stark opposition to the Social Security Act by many claiming that social security was a form of socialism. President Roosevelt and supporters of this newly enacted Tax Act claimed it would free up employment for younger men. Women were also excluded from receiving social security benefits when it was enacted.

Construction began on the United States Department of Justice Building in 1935 at a cost of $10 million to the American taxpayers, which is the value of approximately $216 million today. Construction would not be completed until 1941.

Although the Great Depression had formally ended, American's were recovering from the financial sufferings. But Congress had decided to start yet another costly building project. The Pentagon Building construction began in 1941 and was completed in 1943.

Congress had originally designated $18 million toward its construction, but the cost is estimated to have been between $63 million and $75 million to complete. President Roosevelt was in office and had personally approved construction of the new War Department facility.

WWII And the Payroll Withholding System

It was during WWII that Congress began the payroll-withholding tax system as well as the requirement for estimated quarterly tax payment in hopes of paying for at least half of the cost of WWII.

The Revenue Act of 1942 was signed into law by President Roosevelt on October 21st, 1942. The Revenue Act of 1942 was a means of funding what Congress had hoped would be most of the expenses of World War II.

This Revenue Act would increase the number of Americans who were subject to federal income tax, and it increased taxes overall. The 1942 Revenue Act would decrease the exemption amount married taxpayers were allowed to claim from $1,500 per year to $1,200 per year and decreased the exemption amount for dependents from $400 to $350 per dependent. The Revenue Act also increased tax rates from 10 percent to 19 percent for married couples earning over $2,000 after exemptions. And increased the tax rates from 80 percent to 88 percent for people earning over $200,000 per year after exemptions. The average medium household income was between $2,200 and $4,000 per year at this time.

The 1942 Revenue Act also created an allowance for deductions of medical expenses and investment interest expenses. At this time only the wealthiest Americans benefited from the investment expense deductions. While most Americans recovering from the Great Depression, they were being plagued with the high taxes.

The Victory Tax of 1942 was added to the Revenue Act on December 31st, 1942. This tax provided for a tax of 5 percent on net income earned in excess of $624 annually. Although it was intended to target non-resident aliens earning money inside the continental United States, the language of the Victory Tax Act did not specifically exclude United States citizens already paying income tax. The Victory Tax would be repealed in 1942.

The Current Tax Payment Act of 1943 was signed into law by President Franklin D. Roosevelt on June 9th, 1943. The Tax Payment Act required employers to withhold federal income taxes from employees' wages and remit the taxes to the federal government every quarter.

Congress passed the Individual Income Tax Act in 1944. Signed into law by President Roosevelt, this created an optional standard deduction for taxpayers, in which taxpayers were allowed to deduct a standard deduction of $500 instead of itemizing deduction to arrive at the taxpayers adjusted gross income. Tax rates would then be calculated based on the taxpayers adjusted gross income. It was signed into law May 29th, 1944.

Unfortunately, it also increased tax rates to 23 percent for lower income taxpayers with adjusted gross income below $2,000 and up to 94 percent for taxpayers with adjusted gross income over $200,000. A taxpayer with modest adjusted gross income between $8,000 to $10,000 were paying 37 percent tax.

Post WWII

To help rebuild countries war-torn by WWII, the United State Congress and President Harry S. Truman's administration proposed the European Recovery Program, also known as the Marshall Plan. President Truman signed into law the Economic Cooperation Act of 1948, which provided American assistance to help rebuild European infrastructure and politically stabilize the economy of countries involved in the war. The Marshall Plan would cost the United States taxpayer $17.6 billion from 1948 to 1951. It passed with heavy United States domestic opposition as American citizens were more focused on the United States economy. Americans in opposition to the Marshall Plan resented spending American tax dollars to rebuild foreign countries while the United States was still financially healing itself. But this would be just the beginning of the United States Congress sending taxpayer funds to aid other countries.

In 1950, the amount of payroll subject to social security withholding tax increased from $3,000 to $3,600, and the percentage rate increased on taxpayers from 1 percent to 1.5 percent. Tax rates on American taxpayers increased as well. The lowest tax rate in 1950 was 20 percent for people earning $0 to $2,000, and the top rate was 9 percent for those earning $200,000 or more. The American average household was earning $3,300 and paying 24.6 percent in federal taxes after deduction allowances for the standard deduction or itemized deductions, and exemptions.

During the 1950s, the Bureau of Internal Revenue suffered scandals for corruption and extortion. President Eisenhower initiated his Reorganization Plan, which replaced the patronage system to that of civil service system, He once again changed the name of the Bureau of Internal Revenue to Internal Revenue Service (IRS), in 1953. President Eisenhower based his reorganization plan on a proposal made by President Harry S. Truman. The reorganization plan within the IRS was an attempt to restore the agencies public confidence about the Internal Revenue Service in the public eye.

Beginning in 1955, as part of President Eisenhower's Reorganization Plan, the due date for personal income tax return due dates would change from March 15th to April 15th.

In 1954 Social Security Amendments were introduced by President Eisenhower to provide for a disability insurance program that would provide additional coverage against economic insecurity for the public in years they were not able to work. It provided no cash benefit, but it was intended to prevent a disabled person's retirement and pensions from being exhausted when they were disabled and unable to work.

On August 1st, 1956, the Social Security Act was amended again to include benefits for disabled workers ages 50-64 and disabled adult children.

In September 1960, President Eisenhower signed yet another amendment to the Social Security Act, allowing for benefit payments to be made to disabled persons of any age and their dependent children.

Medicare Hospital Insurance (Medicare) was implemented on July 30th, 1965, by Lindon B. Johnson, adding to the Social Security Act, and extending health care coverage to Americans 65 and older. The payroll withholding rate for working Americans started at .35 percent on the first $6,600 of wages in 1966. The Social Security Administration also responsible for the administration of the new Medicare Insurance. This additional wage withholding would be a total of 4.2 percent on wage earners in the United States. Self-employed workers would pay a total of 6.15 percent on net earnings.

In 1960, under President Eisenhower, Congress allocated money to begin building the United States Housing and Urban Development Building at a cost of $26 million. By today's dollar value, this building ended up costing the American taxpayer over $2.2 billion.

ATF (known as Bureau of Alcohol, Tobacco, and Firearms) would be established in 1972, and become the agency responsible for regulating alcohol tobacco and firearms, relieving the IRS of enforcement and regulation of alcohol and tobacco sales.

Congress passed the Employee Retirement and Income Security Act in 1974. This new law ensured protection for workers' retirement savings. It would set a standard of rules that had to be followed to prevent fiduciary plan administrators from abusing and misusing employee's retirement funds.

The amount of payroll subject to Social Security withholding tax in 1974 had increased to $13,200 and the rate of withholding increased to 4.95 percent. Together with the Medicare Insurance withholding, wage earners would have a total of 5.85 percent on the first $13,200 of wages earned. Self-employed individuals were required to pay 7.9 percent on the first $13,200 of net earnings. Medicare Hospital Insurance tax (Medicare) withholding rate had been increased to .9 percent.

Tax Rates from 1977 to 1981 tax rates ranged between 14 percent for those with adjusted gross income of $2,200 to $2,700 all the way up to 70 percent for taxpayers with adjusted gross income over $100,000, after taking into account the taxpayers' deductions and exemption amounts, of course. Calculating for inflation, wages of $2,200 in 1977 would be the equivalent of approximately $10,757 today.

From 1982 to 1987, rates continued to be 11 percent for taxpayers with adjusted gross income over $2,480 to 50 percent for those with adjusted gross income of $88,270 or more.

It was not until 1988 when median earning taxpayers saw a relief in tax rates. The top tax rate fell to 38.5 percent for taxpayers with adjusted gross income of $54,000 or more.

In 1998, Congress passed the IRS Restructuring and Reform Act, once again reorganizing the IRS in an attempt to align with taxpayers' needs and transforming the IRS into a more customer-based organization. This law expanded taxpayer protections and taxpayer rights outlining a mission for taxpayers receive more professional and courteous services from the Internal Revenue Service. The law also provided for taxpayers have electronic access to their tax accounts.

Congress building and spending projects were far from over though. As frustrating as it may be for many Americans, spending taxpayers' money on excessive government projects has become second nature for Congress. Since the beginning of the formation of our government and tax collection from Americans, there have been many spending and building projects. Too many to name them all. As stated in the beginning, Congress holds the purse of the United States and can spend taxpayer funds as they see fit.

It has not just been building projects that Congress has allocated taxpayer money to that have frustrated millions of Americans, though. Just in 1990 alone, Congress spent $5.1 billion in foreign economic aid for other countries.

In 1995. the amount spent by Congress in foreign economic aid for other countries was $11.2 billion. In the year 2000, the amount spent for aid in foreign countries was $10.8 billion. In 2020 the amount spent to aid foreign countries was a powerful $55.6 billion. These amounts have been embedded in the United States military budget annually, so most Americans never see the money sent to foreign countries.

There have been numerous questions from American taxpayers as to why we are sending so much money to foreign countries and what these countries are doing with our tax dollars.

These foreign financial aid expenditures are in addition to the building projects Congress has spent taxpayers' money on. The building projects never slowed down through the years. For instance, as part of the American Recovery and Reinvestment Act of 2009, Congress spent $1.665 billion for modernization of government general service administration historical buildings.

But I digress, back to taxation subjects. On December 22nd, 2017, President Donald Trump signed into law the 2017 Tax Cut and Jobs Act. This Tax Act was the biggest tax reform since 1986. The 2017 Tax Cut and Jobs Act reduced the number of Americans that would need to itemize tax deductions as it drastically increased the standard deduction for most Americans. It was intended to simplify tax filings for millions of American taxpayers. President Trump has been vocal over the years about wanting to put tax returns on a post card. But this Tax Act did not in any way accomplish that. In fact, it added pages to the common tax return.

The Tax Cut and Jobs Act significantly reduced state and local tax deduction claims for several American taxpayers. There is quite a lot of buzz in the media about taxpayers' concern over this portion of the law called the SALT Deduction. What the SALT Deduction did was limit the amount of property, state, and local taxes people could deduct. The SALT provision limited the amount of combined state taxes, property taxes, and local taxes to a maximum of $10,000 in itemized deductions. It also reduced the amount of mortgage interest that could be deducted for taxpayers that own real estate with mortgages over $750,000.

It also expanded the child credit and decreased marginal tax rates for most taxpayers. It is estimated that 28.5 million Americans benefited from the federal tax changes included in this Tax Act. Although, I have to say that most taxpayers that I prepare taxes for only saw a difference of approximately $100 either way.

The provisions of the 2017 Tax Cut and Jobs Act are due to expire on December 31st, 2025. After the expiration of the 2017 Tax Cut and Jobs Act, the continuation of some or most of these federal tax changes will be up to Congress.

My final point of government expenditures throughout history; most people know and understand that when business owners financially struggle, one of the most common disscisions they make is where to cut costs. When the average taxpayer financially struggles, they also look at where they can reduce or cut costs and expenses. The United States government historically tends to not act in this manner.

WHAT ARE THE CHANCES
OF GETTING AUDITED?

Just as the United States government taxation system has evolved, so has the technology it uses to ensure taxpayers file and pay the appropriate amount in taxes. When the Revenue Act of 1862 was passed, giving the Commissioner of the IRS the power to collect taxes and enforce collection through seizures of property and income, the Internal Revenue did not have a means of direct enforcement. The United States government left it up to the individual states to handle direct enforcement as the state saw fit.

After the Sixteenth Amendment to the Constitution was signed in 1909, the IRS become more resourceful in their tax collection methods. The creation of United States Postal Service and computer systems has assisted in improving the tax collection and enforcement over time. Tax audits are one of the many avenues the Internal Revenue Service uses to enforce compliance.

One of the many tax return compliance methods used by IRS is a computerized scoring system. This system scans tax returns as they are processed by the IRS. This system helps the IRS determine which tax returns that should be selected for manual review or audit.

One of the computerized systems scoring functions is Discriminant Index Function System (DIF) scoring. The DIF rates the tax return for prospective changes that need to be made based on several factors. These factors assist by identifying irregularities on a tax return. The DIF identifies such things as if a dependent has been claimed twice, if there is other duplicate information contained in the tax return, or if the tax return contains credits or deductions that do not make sense. This system also rates a return based on historical IRS experience with other returns that are similar in nature.

Another function of the IRS computerized system uses is the Unreported Income Function scoring DIF (UI DIF) system. This function flags a tax return for unreported income. After the IRS computer system flags a return, the IRS personnel manually review the highest-scoring tax returns. The IRS personnel also look at the type of the flag received by the computer system. At this point, they select some for audit and identify the items on these tax returns that are most likely in need of a manual review.

IRS personnel can choose several options to correct the deficiencies. These options include sending a letter to the taxpayer explaining the changes made to their return, sending a notice to the taxpayer asking for more information, or auditing the return.

The IRS computerized system is constantly becoming more efficient at recognizing issues on tax return. Some tax professionals believe taxpayers will see more IRS correspondence audits and less in-person audits. Correspondence audits allow IRS employees to spend less time on individual audits therefore conduct more audits overall.

The DIF and the UI DIF can also trigger or flag some tax returns to be selected for audit if the tax return involves issues or transactions with other taxpayers' tax returns. Some of these triggers might include a business partner's or investor's tax return that was also selected for audit. Due to the very nature of this aspect of the IRS computerized system, it would be wise to use caution with who you do business with. If your business partners or investors tax return has issues it may have the IRS looking at your tax return, especially if the business partner or investors tax return contains suspicious transactions and deductions. There are several other factors that can create a situation where your tax return is flagged for audit based on what you report or do not report. Let us look at some more obvious items might have the IRS taking a second look at your return.

Unreported Income

We have all heard of people claiming they never report their self-employed earnings to the IRS. And that they have never filed a tax return on that income. People who do this will eventually find themselves in front of the IRS dealing with uncomfortable odds. The IRS is constantly perfecting their methods to find these people.

If you are self-employed, the money you earn from other companies or individuals, is required by law to be reported to the IRS on a form 1099 (Non-Employee Compensation Form) annually. The 1099-Misc or 1099-NEC is required to be filed with the IRS by January 31st each year. Because these forms are required to be filed with the IRS, even if you do not receive a copy of it, as also required by law, the IRS most likely knows relatively quickly you earned this income.

The company or individual paying the taxpayer non-employee compensation is required by law to request your Social Security number or federal identification number on a form W-9. If the taxpayer refuses to provide the payor with the Social Security number or federal identification number, the payor that hired the individual is required to inform the individual that they (the payer) must begin withholding 24 percent backup withholding from any future payments they pay to the taxpayer.

If the taxpayer refuses to provide the company or individual that hired them their Social Security number or federal identification number, the payer should still file the 1099 with the IRS providing the name and address of the individual they hired and write "refused" in the space where the Social Security number or federal identification number would normally go. This still alerts the IRS of the person's name and the amount that person was paid.

Interest you earn over $10 on bank accounts, bonds, other financial accounts are also required to be reported to the IRS annually on a

1099-INT or 1099-DIV. These forms are also filed with the IRS under your social security number or your federal identification number.

All informational returns, such as 1099 and 1098 forms, are entered into the IRS computer system, which uses an Information Returns Processing System (IRP) to match with a taxpayer's return. Information reported to the IRS from third party payers on forms such as 1099's is inputted into the IRS computer system and is then cross-referenced with information reported on an individual's tax return. If the IRS computer system discovers unreported income, the return is forwarded to the examination unit within the IRS. At that point, the taxpayer will receive a letter from the IRS stating the taxpayer had unreported income on their return.

Even if you do not receive a 1099 from the payer, your tax return could be triggered for manual review for other reasons. If the IRS does conduct a manual review of a taxpayer's tax return and there is unreported income, the IRS has the option to audit the taxpayer's return, correct the taxpayer's tax return and notify the taxpayer of the underreported income, or both.

If a taxpayer understates the greater of either the tax required to be reported on their return by 10 percent or more or if the taxpayer understates their income by $5,000 or more, the taxpayer is subject to a substantial understatement penalty. Internal Revenue Code section 6662(d)(1) provides the IRS shall charge the taxpayer a penalty of 20 percent of the understated tax. Even if this is an oversight on the taxpayers' part, it could end up costing more than the taxpayer bargained for.

It is important to note, if you do not carefully track the income you actually receive you could end up paying taxes on money not yet collected from a third-party payer. Cash basis taxpayers, or (taxpayers that report income when they actually receive the income vs. taxpayers that report the income when income earned), make up most taxpayers and highlights the importance of tracking actual income received. This does not include income deposited or anticipated income, but rather income you have in your possession in the taxable year.

To illustrate the importance of tracking actual income received, I will provide one of many examples I have seen. Third-party payers submitted 1099's to the IRS after sending payments to my client end of December, although my client did not receive the money until January of the following year. The IRS received 1099's from third-party payers. Some of the companies that had sent payments to my client did not mail the payments until the end of December and my client had not received the money until the January of the next year. After his tax return was filed, the IRS sent him a notice they had changed his tax return to include $18,000 of income he had not reported on his tax return. We moved forward in filing a tax court petition. Because we could prove that he had not received the income until the next year, the IRS conceded to the originally filed taxable income reported.

Excessive Tax Deductions

Another function the IRS computer system performs when tax returns are processed is an algorithm function process that detects unusual claims, such as large tax deductions, shared dependents claimed on a return, and any other questionable items. Although this system is not perfect, it consistently alerts IRS employees of irregularities that can trigger a manual review by IRS employees.

The IRS audits people for a variety of reasons, but mainly it is to find potential tax revenue from income that was not reported by taxpayers on their tax returns and to look for people claiming deductions in excess or deductions the taxpayer had no right to claim at all. Remember, the IRS is the agency responsible for collecting money to fund the United States government. The potential for unrecovered revenue usually comes in two forms: understated income and overstated deductions. You have been advised of some of the ways the IRS discovers understated income. Let us look at some of the deductions the IRS discovers have been overstated on a tax return and can land your tax return in manual review if you involve yourself in these strategies.

Deducting 100% Business Vehicle Use

The IRS believes that if you use any vehicle for business use, it is highly unusual that you will use this vehicle for business only. If your tax return claims 100 percent business use on your vehicle, this is likely to draw questions from the IRS. This is especially true if you do not have another personal vehicle. I would recommend that you keep very detailed records if you are claiming a high percentage of business use on your personal vehicle. You should keep a contemporaneous daily log on any vehicle you use for business as well as separation of the personal use of that same vehicle.

The log should include the location you drove to/from, the purpose of that travel, the date of the travel, and the mileage for the business purpose, and if you are meeting with customers, the customer's name, and business meeting purpose. I think it bears repeating that driving from your home to your place of business or to your business from your home that mileage is usually considered personal use of that vehicle.

Large Meal Deductions

Claiming an excessive amount of meal deductions can have the IRS performing a manual review of your tax return. This is especially true if you are in the type of business that does not warrant meeting with customers or clients in order to maintain or increase business revenue. Lavish meals will also draw attention from the IRS. Over the years, there have been numerous tax court cases where business owners have claimed an excessive amount of meals and it caused the IRS computer system to flag the tax return.

The IRS does not anticipate a person operating a welding business will incur business meals expenses unless that person also travels to perform welding jobs. They also do not anticipate that a hairdresser will have business meals deductions. When your tax return is prepared, you should try to look at the logical way an IRS auditor will look at it. If you know it does not make sense, then the deduction will not make sense to the IRS as well.

Most business meals deduction is denied in audit and then in tax court for lack of substantiation of the deduction.

Since meals deductions have been suspended until 2025 for employees, this deduction audit trigger commonly focuses on business owners.

Failure to Report Cryptocurrency

All types of cryptocurrencies are hot topics with the IRS these days. Tax professionals are now required to answer the question "**At any time during year, did you receive, sell, send, exchange or otherwise acquire any financial interest in any virtual currency**" within their tax software. The IRS now treats virtual currency on the tax reporting requirement regulations in the same manner it handles other investments, such as stocks and bonds. You must keep extensive records on buying, selling, and transferring cryptocurrency. Failure to keep these detailed records could cause you a lot of headache, time and money straightening it all out with the IRS.

Claiming Hobby Losses as Business Losses

Many people have what they consider a side business. But a side business is not necessarily considered a business for tax purposes even if you are doing it for the purpose of making some extra money. This conversation is one you should have with your tax professional even if you did not make very much money. The problematic issue with having a side business is when people are wanting to deduct expenses for a side business. You cannot deduct any of your expenses from your side business, but you still must report the money on your tax return. Businesses, for tax purposes, are expected to make a profit for three out of five tax years of operation. There are other factors that must be taken into consideration before you can deduct expenses for it to be considered a business for tax purposes as well.

Side businesses are often considered hobbies. Treating a side business or hobby as a business can create audit triggers. This matters more than you would think. Not only because a business can deduct expenses from the business, but businesses can also show a loss and hobbies cannot. The IRS has a list of nine factors they use in determining whether an activity is a legitimate business or a hobby. They consider each case on its own merits. Some of the several factors that are taken into consideration when determining if you are operating a business or a hobby are as follows:

1) You need to keep good business records, such as having a separate business checking account, keeping a formal set of books on your business, and generally running your activity like a business.

2) You must put time and effort into the business as well as spending time marketing, advertising, and other activities to bring in customers and profit.

3) You should show that you anticipate a dependency on the income from this activity for your livelihood for this to be considered a business, not that you will immediately have a dependency on the business for your livelihood.

4) If you do have losses, you should show that your business losses are beyond your control or are losses that are typical startup losses.

5) If you do show a loss or little profit, you should show that you are making changes in your operations to improve your profits. Changes in operations could include things like cutting some

expenses that produce poor results or tend to not produce results at all. After all, you are not the United States government.

6) You should start a business in which you have the expertise to operate. If you do not have the expertise, you must show that you are willing hire competent business advisors to make the business profitable.

7) Show that you have been successful in similar businesses in the past.

8) You should show that you can make a profit in some years and if so, how much? Preparing a business profit model helps a quite a bit with this aspect.

9) You should show that you expect to make a profit in the future if you are now showing a loss.

None of these factors are given more influence than others when determining if you are operating a business or if you are participating in a hobby. But to be a little safer in the audit arena it is recommended that you meet at least 5 or of the 9 factors. Even if you do meet 5 or more out of the 9 factors, you will need to show that the time you put into operating the business and the way you conduct your business as well as your income from other sources of income can substantiate that you are operating a business. If you are working a full-time job and just operating your business part-time, that will most likely draw greater scrutiny from the IRS.

Example: You are employed as an arborist for ABC Company who receives a W-2 wages of $70,000 a year for your work with ABC Company. You also work for yourself on the side building garden fencing. The work you do on the side building garden fencing has a net loss of $3050.00 for the prior three years. The IRS might consider this a hobby even though the work is hard tedious work. If you do not spend adequate time and effort in building this side business up to make a profit in the future, this could work against you in audit.

Keep in mind, to be considered a hobby the work does not necessarily have to be something that you simply enjoy doing. It can be something you work very hard at when you are doing the work on the hobby.

Home Based Businesses

The IRS believes taxpayers that operate a home-based business often deduct their expenses improperly, deduct expenses they should not, and do not accurately track their expenses. Tracking a percentage of utilities, home maintenance, and home repairs are common errors for home-based business owners. The IRS also believes that home-based business owners have a bad habit of commingling personal funds with business funds.

This belief is due to experience from taxpayers who ride the tight rope and deduct things they should not do to get a better tax return outcome. Realistically, home-based business is a common area for red flags with the IRS.

There are very specific rules for home office deductions, i.e., people who run their businesses out of their homes. Many people try to claim multi-purpose areas for a home office deduction. Be careful with this idea if you want to stay off the IRS radar.

If you are operating a home-based business, be sure to keep your business income and expenses separate from your personal income and expenses. Understand what is considered business in nature and what is considered personal in nature in the view of the IRS.

Tax Professionals get asked a wealth of questions every year about home-office deductions from taxpayers. Another reason this is an area that is an audit trigger, is unfortunately some unscrupulous or unknowledgeable tax professionals get their clients into trouble with the IRS. It is also an area where many tax myths derive every year based on what taxpayers have heard from friends, relatives, and co-workers, and even tax professional.

Self-Employed Taxpayers

Self-employed taxpayers are eligible to tax deductions that the average W-2 wage earner does not get to take advantage of. Expenses for running a business, including home-office deductions and business mileage are deducted from your self-employed gross earnings to determine your taxable income.

The IRS computerized scoring system, the DIF, also gives tax returns with self-employment a relatively high DIF score. The system scores items such as deductions that are above normal compared to the same deductions for similar businesses.

The IRS is alerted to those claiming deductions that have a higher-than-average ratio versus reported income for like kind professions. This is one of the reason profession codes are entered onto each self-employed Schedule C tax return form. It gives the IRS the type of business you are operating, so they may compare income and expenses for the same type of business in your area.

Example: Taxpayer A is self-employed as a computer repair technician, and he spends approximately 20% of his income on travel each year, which is the average travel expenses reported by others in this profession in his area. Taxpayer B is also a computer repair technician, and he spends 35% of his income on travel for the same year. Because taxpayer B spent 15% more of his income on travel expenses, he can probably expect the IRS to take a closer look at his return.

Claiming Earned Income Credit

Earned Income Tax Credit is a very common and popular tax credit taken by lower income taxpayers. The use of this tax credit can create a trigger for a tax audit because it is so often abused. It has become a higher priority audit trigger for the IRS in recent years.

This credit is refundable and taxpayers claiming this credit can receive a refund from the IRS if the credit is more than their tax liability. This is also one of the reasons that Earned Income Tax Credit claims are more likely to be subject to an audit. The IRS does not like handing out fraudulent money. It makes them look bad. This is especially true after the discovery that the IRS paid out billions in erroneous refunds since the credit was added to tax code.

It has been recognized that this has become a popular tax credit for fraudulent tax preparers and tax scammers to get money out of the IRS that they had no right to collect. The fraudulent claims of this credit operate somewhat like identity theft. Have you ever filed your taxes and been notified that one of your children has already been claimed? It is possible this is one of the reasons that happened to you. It only makes sense the IRS takes a closer look at returns claiming the Earned Income Credit. This also a very good reason to keep your own information safeguarded in addition to keeping your children's information safe.

Cash-Based Businesses

Operating a mostly cash business – like salons, bars, restaurants, and car washes -- can also give you a higher Discriminant Index Function System (DIF) score. Most cash transaction-based businesses raise suspicion with the IRS, especially if you generally report a lower income than similar business in your area.

If you are self-employed and file a Schedule C tax return and you report mostly cash income and expenses, the IRS generally also wants to know if you are understating your income or overstating your deductions. So, if you do run a cash business and pay for quite a few small expenses in cash be sure to keep those cash receipts. Do not try to report unusual deductions for your profession unless you can prove the expense were genuinely 100 percent necessary for your business and you actually spent the money on expenses for the business.

The IRS will also "score" you higher and flag your return if your lifestyle is such that you reported lower business income and your total income from all sources after business expenses isn't enough to support your lifestyle, yourself, and your family.

Math Errors Or Typos

This one is not really a big trigger, but it can throw your return into a stack for manual review. It rarely triggers an audit, but it never hurts to work with a professional accountant or online tax preparation system instead of attempting to do a manual tax return to avoid these types of errors and avoid the headache all together.

Using Unscrupulous Tax Preparer

Although most purported tax professionals with an IRS Preparer Tax Identification Number (PTIN) are authorized to prepare federal tax returns, not all of them are ethical or of good moral character. The important difference in the types of practitioners is rights they have been given to represent your return. The following is a short summary of three different tax professional licensee categories that are generally what you should look for based your tax planning, preparation, and representation needs:

Enrolled Agents – Licensed by the IRS and federally recognized to prepare taxes, represent taxpayers, provide tax planning, and provide tax consulting throughout the United States, the District of Columbia, and the U.S. territories.

Certified Public Accountants – Licensed by individual state boards of accountancy and federally recognized to prepare taxes, represent taxpayers, provide tax planning, and provide tax consulting throughout the United States, the District of Columbia, and U.S. territories.

Attorneys – Licensed by states, the District of Columbia, or their designees, such as the attorney's state bar agency. Licensed to represent clients in most court settings. Federally recognized to prepare taxes, represent taxpayers, provide tax planning, and provide tax consulting throughout the United States, the District of Columbia, and the U.S. territories.

An important thing to note, if a CPA, an enrolled agent, or a tax attorney made an error in the preparation of your return, you have a defense against penalties that may be imposed on you by the IRS. The IRS may waive some or all the penalties if you can prove that you provided all the pertinent information to have your tax return prepared accurately, completely, and truthfully and you relied upon their knowledge to properly follow tax law in the preparation of your return.

But this defense is only allowed to subvert penalties and occasionally the interest. It does not prevent you from paying the taxes you are legally liable for even if the taxes were improperly calculated by the CPA, the enrolled agent, or the tax attorney. And realistically, you would have paid the tax anyway.

All three of these tax professional types may represent clients before the administrative processes of the IRS. However, if you are unfortunate enough to go beyond the IRS with tax issues and might have to defend your tax position in tax court, only attorneys and United States tax court practitioners may represent clients in tax court.

Why does any of this information matter? Use of an unscrupulous tax preparer might put you in the position where it is necessary for you to go to tax court to defend your own tax return. This situation is similar to having an untrustworthy business partner. On more than on one occasion, an unscrupulous tax preparer's returns have been audited. After the IRS has audited the preparer and recognized some illicit tax patterns, they look at returns the preparer has filed for clients. If some of the returns prepared by the tax preparer resulted in extensive changes, the IRS then looks at more of the returns filed by the preparer. The IRS has a method to statistically look for patterns in the returns that a tax preparer has worked on.

Regardless of how the tax professional gets caught, you do not want to be one of their clients regardless the refund amounts they "get for you." Ask yourself this question: Is the additional $1,000 refund you received this year worth potentially spending thousands of dollars in penalties, interest, and representation charges if you get audited? Odds are these later charges will be double or even triple the amount of the additional refund you received in tax refunds.

Tax preparers, both unlicensed and licensed have been a high-priority target of the IRS for many years now because of the unethical and unscrupulous practices used by some. I run across the tax court cases of these scoundrels every so often. In fact, the IRS Office of Professional Responsibility releases a bulletin every quarter listing tax professional that have had disciplinary sanctions brought against them for a variety of reasons. One of the most recent quarters showed there were 16 tax professionals that were sanctioned. Of those, 10 were CPAs, three were attorneys, and three were enrolled agents. The IRS does not publish a list of unlicensed preparers that have had charges brought against them because the IRS does not have authority over unlicensed preparers like they do licensed preparers. These are the people were caught and sanctioned because they are licensed. Imagine the number of tax preparers that have not had disciplinary actions brought against them.

Before I go further, I should say not all people who proport to be a "tax professional" are held to the same standards of others. enrolled agents, CPAs, and tax attorneys are very good examples of tax professionals whose feet are held to the fire with tax returns they prepare for others. These types of professional tax return preparers risk being fined a great deal of money for inaccurate preparation of tax returns. A blatant disregard for tax regulation is not only frowned upon, but results in tax professionals holding these types of credentials to have disciplinary actions by their licensing authorities.

Ignorance of the law is never an acceptable excuse for someone claiming to be a professional. CPAs, enrolled agents, and tax attorneys are required to complete continuing education every year to renew their licensees. Unlicensed preparers are not required to obtain annual continuing tax education. Most licensed tax professionals also carry Errors and Omissions insurance if mistakes are made on any tax returns prepared by them. Errors and Omissions insurance can cover the taxpayers' penalties and interest if the tax professional made errors on a tax return. It does not usually cover any fines or penalties from the IRS charged to the tax professional.

How do you know if you are using a fraudulent tax preparer? One obvious sign is that if it sounds too good to be true, it probably is. Look for things like, does your tax preparer offer service fees based on a refund amount? Does your tax preparer often get you a large tax refund when you have little or no documentation to support deductions? Is your tax return unsigned by the preparer? Does your tax preparer offer a larger refund then their competitors without looking at your documentation? Does your tax preparer advertise they can "sell" you dependents? Yes, there have been tax preparation offices that have done this. If you answered "yes" to any of these questions, you should seriously closely scrutinize your return and maybe be looking for another tax return preparer. The IRS Criminal

Investigation Division (CID) has been increasingly pursuing unscrupulous return preparers to enforce compliance from the tax preparation community.

You should also be aware that if your tax preparer is exaggerating deductions for you, they most likely are doing the same thing for their other tax clients as well as themselves. These indications give you something to think about when using anyone who professes to be a professional tax preparer and displays any of these characteristics. You are ultimately responsible for what is on your return. You sign the tax return stating under penalty of perjury that the information on the tax return is true and accurate to the best of your knowledge. Not all tax professionals are created equal.

In 2013 the IRS litigated a lawsuit over the subject of purported professional tax preparers who held no licensing or continuing education requirements. The petitioners of the case were preparing tax returns for taxpayers without the licensing to do so. The case was *Loving v. Internal Revenue Serv.,742 F.3d 1013)*. The plaintiffs were a collective of tax preparers who claimed that the burden of annual continuing tax education and being licensed by the IRS would drive them out of business. The court concluded that the IRS did not have the authority to require a license and continuing education from people preparing tax returns for others for money. The court stated it would be up to Congress to pass a law requiring that tax return preparers become licensed nation-wide and obtain continuing education every year.

There are some individual states that require a tax preparation license. What does this mean to the taxpayer? It is essential to question whether your tax professional undergoes annual continuing education to keep current with tax laws so they may prepare your tax return accurately.

One recent example of an unscrupulous tax preparation office is the case of Petra Gomez, an unlicensed tax preparer convicted April 2021, who was prosecuted for conspiracy to defraud the government and tax evasion. Her sister and business partner, Jakeline Lumucso, was convicted in November 2020, for conspiracy to defraud the government. Both women, from Orlando, Florida, fraudulently prepared tax returns for migrants between January 2012 to June 2016.

The court ordered Gomez and Lumucso to pay $24,940,495 in restitution to the IRS. Gomez was ordered to pay an additional $510,999 to the IRS for tax evasion on her own tax return. Gomez and Lumucso conspired to defraud the IRS by submitting more than 16,000 false tax returns. In addition to filing fraudulent tax returns for others, Gomez's own tax return resulted in nearly $25 million in fraudulent tax refunds.

The two of them created over five different tax preparation companies throughout Florida in other people's names. This is the classic example of unlicensed fraudulent tax preparers to avoid. Rather their clients had knowledge of being a party to the fraudulent tax scheme is another question. The Special Agent in Charge, Brian Payne of IRS Criminal Investigation, was quoted saying "Putting abusive return preparers out of business is a top priority for IRS."1

You can look up stories about these types of tax preparers by searching on-line for "tax preparer convicted" yourself to see what I am talking about. You should do everything to avoid these types of tax preparers to stay out of the IRS's line of fire. You should also watch out if the tax preparer indicated on your tax return that the return was "self-prepared." This is also good indications that you might be dealing with an unscrupulous tax return preparer.

But without Congressional interference, these unscrupulous tax return preparers will not be put out of business or be barred from fraudulently preparing tax returns for others for profit.

I cannot say enough about the dangers of using a person who prepares fraudulent tax returns for others. I am talking about tax preparers who are aggressive with deductions that go well beyond the "grey" area of tax law. Or those who skim numbers off the books for business owners to produce lower taxable income. And of course, let us not forget about those that are just simply crooks and scammers.

The common taxpayer is fearful of landing in the IRS's radar. But the prudent taxpayer makes certain all their income is claimed, all their deductions and credits are legitimate, and all of their tax documents are properly prepared in order to avoid extensive review of their tax returns.

MOST COMMON TAX MYTHS
YOU MAY HAVE HEARD

I once had a tax instructor say, "when you think of taxes, think greed." This could be why so many taxpayers try "gray" areas of tax law to save money on their taxes. Some even go so far breaching the "gray" areas. The simple explanation for taxpayers getting into trouble could be that tax laws are so complicated taxpayers do not understand they have inadvertently prepared their taxes improperly. This is also one of the most significant reasons why it is so important to be sure you use a professional tax preparer that is up to date on current tax laws.

Taxpayers talk to friends, relatives, and co-workers about taxes when they are looking for ways to pay less taxes and save money. I firmly believe this is why tax professionals get so many questions from taxpayers that are just plain tax myths. But a conscientious taxpayer talks to his or her tax professional before getting themselves into a bind with the IRS.

As a tax professional having spent over 28 years in the industry, I can tell you there are fewer things more irritating than having people say "my buddy told me I can write off -------". *Free* advice from a person that does not advise on taxes occupationally can lead taxpayers into troubled waters with things they have *heard* from others that is simply myths. If the person giving you *free* advice has advanced knowledge about a subject, that person would most likely be making money in their own life for that advice.

It is not uncommon for me to have several questions every year from clients about a tax *loophole* they heard about from another person that is not a tax professional.

Now that I have shared my experience with you about people not in the professional tax advising industry and their tax advice to others, let me share some of the most common misconstrued, mythical tax questions and misunderstandings I have been asked and how I respond to them.

Q: If I did some work on "the side" and was not sent a 1099, do I still have to report the income on my taxes?

YES. Unconditionally do not under report your income because you may believe there is no way the IRS will ever know, but potential future audits will expose this seemingly innocent white lie.

Internal Revenue Code (I.R.C) section 61(a) defines Taxable Income as gross income from whatever source derived. This includes income earned from a "side business."

When the IRS conducts an audit, some of items the IRS has the authority to ask for are your bank statements or banking transactions. If that "side work money" has reached your bank account, you will have to explain where that money came from. Even if the money never reaches your bank account the IRS has other means and methods for finding out if you have unreported income. The IRS can request documentation on things like payment receipts of bills you pay, purchase receipts for assets you own, and receipts for utilities paid. The purpose of asking for these types of documents is to determine if the taxpayer's lifestyle can be supported by the income reported on their tax return. This is true even though an economic or financial status audit is disallowed UNLESS the IRS has a reasonable indication the taxpayer has unreported income.

Aside from bank records, the person that paid you the money might have filed a 1099 with the IRS even if you did not receive a copy of the 1099. For the payer, the fines, penalties, and questions asked by the IRS for not filing a 1099 for work rendered can be uncomfortable. I.R.C. (Internal Revenue

Code) section 162(a) requires the payer to substantiate all ordinary and necessary business expenses claimed on the payor's tax return. This means they must show proof that they paid you for your work for the benefit of their business and it was necessary to pay you for the work. Some states, such as Oregon, have been known to disallow the deduction if the payer did not file a 1099 for services rendered.

I was recently contacted by a client whose husband had never received a 1099 for "side-work" he believed was under-the-table income. The client's husband worked for his stepbrother's business and made some extra income. The client's husband believed his stepbrother's business would not report it to the IRS, and therefore he would not need to report it on his taxes The stepbrother did file a 1099 on the money he had paid my client's husband and the IRS said that both spouses equally owed additional taxes, plus penalties for underreporting and interest because they filed a joint tax return. When the tax return was filed, the wife did not know that husband had received this additional income.

When a joint tax return is filed, both spouses are deemed to owe the tax on the income regardless of who earned the money. There is no defending the underreported income with the IRS. The only option for the spouse who did not earn the income is to file what is called an Innocent Spouse Relief. This separates the income on the jointly filed tax return as though the tax-payers had filed separate tax returns. It is very difficult to obtain a favorable determination for an Innocent Spouse Relief request. To qualify for consideration the innocent spouse must meet very stringent guidelines.

The two main takeaways from this: 1) always claim money you have earned on your tax return if it is taxable income; and 2) when filing a joint tax return, be sure you know what your spouse has earned and make sure it is reported on your joint tax return.

Q: If I have a business in-home office, what can I deduct for my home office: fine art, master bedroom remodel, new hot tub, or a swimming pool?

This is another one of those tax myths that gets grossly misinterpreted. If you abuse your deductions on this issue, you may find yourself drowning in debt with the IRS for that swimming pool or you might have to sell that fine art to pay your tax bill (plus penalties and interest of course).

How will the IRS know? I.R.C. (Internal Revenue Code) section 7605 and 7602 authorizes the IRS to hold an examination audit at such time and place fixed by the IRS as are reasonable given under the circumstances. So, to put it more clearly, the IRS does have the authority to request an appointment to observe the physical location you claim as your home office.

If you have a home office, you should pay careful attention and ask your tax preparation professional specific questions about the deductibility of your home office. Keep in mind, this is also a popular audit area for the IRS because of the Discriminant Index Function System (DIF) scoring system. If you exaggerate the deductions for home office, the IRS computers system can flag the return.

The term "home" for purposes of this deduction as defined by I.R.C. 280A(f)(1) includes a house, apartment, condominium, mobile home, boat, or similar property which provides basic living accommodations. It can also include separate structure on the property such as an unattached garage, studio, barn, or greenhouse if it is used exclusively for business use.

Another common misused home-office deduction is **deducting part of your mortgage payment on your tax return**. You should be able to deduct **part** of your mortgage interest or rental payments (if you do not own the home), your property taxes, property insurance, utilities, repairs, maintenance. If you do own the home, you should also be able to take depreciation on the portion of the home used for business purposes. That is, if you satisfy the certain qualifications to take the home office deduction.

I have a couple of tax clients that I still do not understand why they do not have a rental loss when they charge rent that is equal to or less than their mortgage payment.

Any portion of a home used as a rental property such as an Airbnb, or bed and breakfast does NOT qualify as a "home" and, therefore, does not qualify for a home office deduction.

There are two primary conditions that need to be met to qualify for the home office deductions:

The portion claimed as a home office must be used exclusively for conducting business on a regular basis.

I.R.C. section 280A(c)(1) specifically limits a taxpayer who uses an extra room as an office, business storage, customer conference room, etc., and is used to also run their business. The business owner might be able take a home office deduction for that extra room so long as it is used both regularly and exclusively in the business.

In other words, the extra room cannot also be used as a "spare bedroom" for guests, etc.

The home you are using for business use must be the taxpayer's primary place of business.

A taxpayer can also meet this requirement if administrative or management activities are conducted at the home office and there is no other location to perform these duties. Therefore, someone who conducts business outside of their home but also uses part of their home to conduct business on a regular basis may still qualify for a home office business deduction even if the home office is not the taxpayer's principal place of business. This can be true if they regularly meet clients or customers in their home office location or the home office location is a separate structure used for meeting clients on a regular basis.

Example: You are a bookkeeper, and you operate your business out of your home office. You meet with clients at their home, the client's office, or some other location but you do all the main bookkeeping activities at your home office. You will qualify for the home office deduction if you also qualify for the exclusive use of the home office area.

You can use one of two methods to calculate your home office expense deduction:

You can use the <u>simplified method</u> by deducting $5 per square foot for business use of the home, but you are limited to a maximum size of 300 square feet and a maximum deduction $1,500.

One of my tax clients insists that his spare bedroom is his home office, simply because he meets with customers there Since I have been to his "home office", I also know that there is a bed, children's toys, and a crib in the same room. Because the home office is utilized for more than work, the function of the space does not meet the requirements of the home office deduction.

Or you can use the regular method where you deduct your home office space based on the percentage of the home devoted to business use over the total square footage of the entire home. With this method you can deduct the home office use percentage of indirect expenses such as home maintenance, home repairs, mortgage interest, property taxes, etc.

Example: Your total home square footage is 1,500 square feet. Your home office is 300 square feet, (300/1500=20%). Your entire home's maintenance for the year was $395.00. You can take $79.00 ($395.00 x 20%=$395.00) as an indirect expense.

Home office expenses that often get overlooked are the percentage of general repairs, maintenance, lawn care, and upkeep on your home. You may be able to deduct a percentage of these deductions per the square footage of the home office.

I caution you by saying do not confuse this with widely misunderstood myths about deducting fine art you decorate your living room with or the replacement of appliances in your kitchen that have nothing to do with conducting business in your home office. You may want to purchase a mini refrigerator for your home office so you can offer refreshments to your clients who come to visit. I used to have a mini refrigerator in my home office. I did often offer my clients a beverage if the meeting was going to take some time, but I was careful to not use that mini refrigerator to keep my personal meals or snacks in. Clients would ask me about the mini refrigerator, and I would joke and tell them that if I offer them an alcohol beverage when they come to pick up their tax return it is not usually good news.

I have clients tell me all the time that some friend has a tax professional that allowed them to deduct 100 percent for a new sidewalk to the main entrance of their home. Or the (friend) taxpayer has been allowed a deduction for building a guest house on their property. You will need to use common sense when deducting expenses for the home office deductions. Remember, if you wave a red flag, you are risking that the IRS will see that flag.

Q: If I use my personal vehicle for my business as a self-employed person, or partner in a partnership, it is considered a company vehicle, and can my business deduct the vehicle?

In short--NO. Even though you can usually deduct either your **vehicle business mileage or a percentage of your business vehicle actual expenses**, the vehicle itself does not belong to your company if it is not titled to your company. This becomes problematic when business owner wants to make their vehicle payments from their business bank account. This causes a great deal of confusion to taxpayers when your tax professional has to subtract those vehicle payments from the business expenses they calculated.

Taxpayers tend to misunderstand that not all of their vehicle expenses or vehicle mileage is 100 percent deductible unless their vehicle is used 100 percent for business and all vehicle business expenses are properly substantiated. I.R.C. section 162(a) states you cannot expense 100 percent of the vehicle usage for business. I.R.C. is somewhat specific in reference to deductions of business expenses. Only expenses that are ordinary and necessary in carrying on any trade or business are deductible as business expenses. This is true even though what the Internal Revenue Code states is ordinary and necessary business expenses seldom agree with what the taxpayer thinks is ordinary and necessary business expenses.

Traveling from one business location to another work location is considered business travel and can be deducted as business travel expenses if there a legitimate business purpose. If the taxpayer is traveling from the taxpayer's residence, which is considered the taxpayer's principal place of business within the meaning of I.R.C. section 280A(c)(1)(A), the taxpayer may deduct travel expense in traveling from the work location to another work location within the same trade or business. If you do not fit within these rules, traveling to and from your home, and other personal vehicle travel expenses are personal in nature and therefore, not ordinary, or necessary to conduct your business. Partners in a Partnership are treated similarly to self-employed persons for vehicle expense deductions.

Example: You have an office that is in a different location from your home. You use your personal vehicle (vehicle #1) to travel to your main office away from your home, and you use another vehicle (vehicle #2) to do all your business-related travel for the day, drive back to your main office and park vehicle #2 at your office. You use vehicle #1 to travel home. If you never use vehicle #2 for any non-business-related purpose, you can then deduct 100 percent of the vehicle mileage or vehicle actual expenses of vehicle #2.

One of my clients is a specialty food shop owner. She only owns one vehicle and uses it regularly for her business to buy products for her shop. She drives the same vehicle to work and home. This client also uses this same vehicle to pick her children up from day-care, make personal trips to the grocery store, and run personal errands after work. She pays all of her vehicle expenses from her business account, including her car payment. Since this customer does not track her mileage specific to business use, she is not able to make use of her vehicle as a business expense. This could be easily remedied with a carefully managed Business Use Mileage Log.

If you have a corporation that has a company vehicle used for business that is also used for personal use, you are required to track your personal use of the vehicle and claim the fair market lease value of the personal use percentage and the personal use expenses such as gas as an employee W-2 addition to your wages. Personal use includes commuting mileage to and/or from your personal residence.

If you take actual expenses for business use of the vehicle instead of the federal standard mileage rate, you can also be allowed to depreciate the business use percentage of the cost of that vehicle in addition to deducting gas, oil, maintenance, repairs, etc. You are allowed a percentage based on the business use percent of the vehicle.

Example: You choose to take actual expenses of the vehicle instead of the standard mileage on that vehicle. You spent $20,000 on a new car for your self-employed business. You use the car for business purposes 75 percent of the time. If you were to claim depreciation and actual expenses for the business use of the car you could take Section 179 depreciation deduction (which means you want to write off the maximum amount of the car in year of purchase). You could take a depreciation deduction of $15,000 ($20,000 × 0.75) on your tax return, plus 75 percent of the actual expenses for gas, oil, maintenance, repairs, tires, and insurance. But I will caution you on this. If you sell or trade that same vehicle within the next five years, you will have to add back the accelerated depreciation you took as income the year you sell or trade this vehicle. A typical automobile depreciates over a five-year period. If you deduct more in the first year and later sell or trade the vehicle, that depreciation has been deducted immediately, not over the prescribed five-year period.

Tip: If you are a shareholder and an employee of an S Corporation, you can create an accountable reimbursement plan that is non-discriminatory. This allows the S Corporation to reimburse employees the federal standard mileage rate for the business use of their personal vehicles. The S Corporation is then allowed to write off the reimbursement for the mileage they paid to employees/ S Corporation shareholder.

To have a proper accountable reimbursement plan, it must be non-discriminatory. This means that if you reimburse the shareholder employees of the S Corporation for their business-related mileage, and only if the business-related mileage is substantiated, the S Corporation should also make the reimbursement available to other employees. There should be language within the accountable reimbursement plan that requires a business use milage log be kept contemporaneously and regularly, then submitted to the S Corporation within a reasonable time.

Q: If I travel for business and visit a relative or am vacationing part of the time I am traveling, I can deduct the entire travel, right?

This particular deduction is widely misused, confused, and abused.

I.R.C. section 162(a)(2) explains that business travel expense deductions that are allowed if the travel is ordinary and necessary, as long as the expenses are not lavish or extravagant in nature, and the travel is for your business or your profession. You need to establish a business purpose to take a business travel deduction. You can also not deduct travel that are primarily for personal purposes.

If you travel for anything other than for business purposes, the travel fares and expenses you pay for your traveling are personal expenses as are the meals and lodging.

Unfortunately, this includes traveling for your employer if you are a W-2 wage earner.

If you travel to a destination and you engage in both business and personal activities, your traveling expenses to and from such destination are deductible only if the trip is related primarily to your trade or business. If the trip is primarily personal in nature, even if you engage in some business activities while traveling it is considered personal in nature and is not deductible. However, you can be allowed to allocate travel related expenses to and from a business purpose destination, such as cab fare to a client's office or location while traveling for personal purposes if you properly document the business only travel expenses, business purpose, business location, etc.

Example: You spend three weeks in Hawaii. One week was spent on activities that are directly related to your trade or business, but for the additional two weeks in Hawaii, you were on vacation. The trip will be considered primarily personal in nature if you do not establish there was a primary business purpose. With this example, only a portion of the expenses directly related to the business purpose, one third of the expenses, will be deductible as business-related travel expenses. You must clearly document the business portion of expenses or the business deduction for your entire trip can be denied.

A couple of years ago, one of my clients took his entire family to Hawaii on vacation. He paid all of the vacation expenses from his business account. He told me that he was probing the market in Hawaii for expansion while he was on vacation. Because he did not keep records of his business purpose expenses, he was not allowed to deduct any of the expenses. All of the money spent was considered personal in nature and non-deductible. Simply put, there needs to be a reasonable effort in separating purchases and expenses that are personal in nature or directly related to business needs before a case can be made that expenses are deductible.

When your spouse accompanies you on a business trip, expenses for your spouse's travel may not be deductible unless it can be adequately shown that the spouse's presence on the trip has a bona fide business purpose. The spouse performing light duties for the business, such as organizing your notes, does not cause the spouses expenses to qualify as deductible business expenses. An example of your spouse's performance would be if your spouse is your business partner and is attending a continuing education conference with you. The same rules apply to any other members of the taxpayer's family who accompany you on a trip.

Traveling expenses

Deductible traveling expenses include things such as: travel fares, meals and lodging, and expenses incident to travel. Expenses for baggage fees, dry cleaning or laundry expenses, business calls, costs for use of fax machines or other communication devices, computer rental fees, and tips you pay are all examples of allowable business travel expenses.

Travel that you do not pay for is not deductible as business travel expense. In other words, for example, if you receive a free travel ticket or you are riding free as a result of a frequent traveler, ride-share, or similar program, your cost in the travel expense for this is zero.

Expenses paid for you to attend a convention or other meeting may be reasonable ordinary and necessary business expense depending upon the facts and circumstances. The deduction allowance for such expenses will depend upon if there is a sufficient relationship between you in your trade or business, and your attendance at the conference or convention. In other words, you need to ask yourself if the convention or conference attendance is advancing the interests of your trade or business. If the convention is for political, social or other purposes unrelated to your trade or business, the expenses may not deductible. There are special rules that apply to conventions held outside North America.

You may also qualify for business deductions for things such as shipping samples or display material between your regular and temporary work locations.

You can deduct actual expenses or the standard mileage rate, as well as business-related tolls and parking fees as a business expense deduction. If you rent a car, you can deduct only the business-use portion for the rental car expenses.

You are allowed to use standard meals allowance instead of keeping records of your actual meal expenses for business related non-reimbursed business meals if the meals and/or the travel have a business-related purpose. The standard meals allowance will vary depending on your travel location. The standard meals allowance for travel areas can be found in IRS Publication 463. The deduction for business meals is generally limited to 50% of the unreimbursed cost.

Q: What can I deduct for client and business-related entertainment?

Unfortunately, this deduction has been so badly abused that it has been eliminated by the Tax Cut and Job Act of 2017. The act disallows a deduction for any activity generally considered to be entertainment, amusement, or recreation, any membership dues for clubs organized for business, pleasure, recreation, or other social purposes, or any activity related to the use of a facility in connection with any of the above items.

The Tax Cut and Job Act of 2017 eliminates the prior 50% business deduction for entertainment, amusement or recreation that is related to the active conduct of the taxpayer's trade or business.

Prior to the elimination of business-related entertainment, taxpayers' abuse of this deduction was glaring. There were many tax court cases on business-related entertainment prior to its elimination. Some taxpayers were claiming deductions for the operation of the taxpayer personal fishing boat, claiming they were entertaining clients on their boat. Other taxpayers were claiming deductions for memberships to golf resorts.

Even professionals in the tax industry that should have known better have found themselves in deep water with these types of deductions, claiming they were entertaining their clients when in reality the expenses were personal in nature.

Although taking business deductions for "entertaining clients" on a fishing boat or golf course has always been in poor judgement, gone are the days of thinking you could take your clients fishing to thank them for their business and deducting the trip.

Q: If I trade in a piece of equipment and buy a replacement piece of equipment, I do not have to pay taxes on the equipment I traded in, right?

I have gotten this type of question from quite a few of my clients that have been in business long enough to remember the older tax law treatments. Current tax laws no longer afford such favorable tax treatment to taxpayer business assets.

Example: Under old tax law, a farmer could trade in farm equipment and recognize no gain or loss on the trade. For example, assume a farmer has an old combine worth $60,000 that has been completely depreciated. The farmer trades it in for a new combine worth $100,000. The $60,000 trade value was essentially ignored, and the tax cost basis of the new combine is simply $40,000 (the net cash paid).

I receive calls every year from a few clients that trade in business equipment and I don't know about it until I prepare their taxes. These clients never prepare for the capital gains tax they have to pay for the trade in on their equipment. One of the more popular types of equipment I see clients trade in is their business vehicle.

This was the case with a real estate professional last year. This client trades in their 100 percent business use vehicle every 4-5 years because of the mileage the client puts on the vehicle. When the client told me they had traded in the old vehicle for a newer vehicle half-way through the year, they were surprised to hear that I needed to know the trade in value they received for the older vehicle. The trade-in value of the older vehicle is subject to capital gains tax because it is treated as though they had sold the vehicle.

I.R.C. section 1231, under the current tax laws, clearly states the sale or exchange of business equipment is a taxable transaction and must be reported on your return as a Long- Term Capital Gains or Ordinary Income (if held longer than 1 year). If property is held for less than 1 year, it must be reported as a Short-Term Capital Gain or as Ordinary Income under I.R.C 1245. This can be true even if you use your old equipment as a trade-in for the newer equipment.

Do not be fooled thinking you can get around the taxation of your transaction that easily. Other factors that may determine the gain on your trade-in or sale of equipment are things such as the amount you originally paid for the equipment you are selling or trading in, the type of equipment you are selling, and the amount of depreciation you have already taken on the older equipment. If you have fully depreciated the equipment, of course your basis in the equipment (the original cost minus depreciation) would be zero.

However, the good news is that with the Tax Cut and Job Act of 2017, the replacement equipment you purchased might be eligible to be completely written off in the year of purchase through bonus depreciation or section 179 depreciation deduction if the equipment is used in your trade or business. Using either of these methods of depreciation may reduce and, in some cases, completely offset the gain from the sale or trade in of the older equipment. These options will remain in effect for equipment replacement until 2025, or of course until Congress changes the law.

Example: Sam trades old office breakroom appliances for newer appliances in his office building breakroom. The older appliances have a fair market value (trade value) of $3,000 and the new appliances have a fair market value of $10,000. The older appliances have been fully depreciated and have zero remaining cost basis. Under the old tax law, Sam would depreciate the fair market value of $7,000 paid on the trade of the newer appliances. No gain would be recognized on the trade value of $3,000 of the older appliances. Under the current tax laws, Sam will recognize a gain of $3,000 on the trade of the appliances. He will then depreciate the full $10,000 cost of the new appliances using regular depreciation, bonus depreciation, Section 179 depreciation, or any combination thereof. With the ability to use bonus depreciation and Section 179 depreciation, Sam will be able to reach the same outcome as he would of under the old tax law.

Q: If owned and lived in my house for two out of five years, rented out the entire house and then sold my it, I don't have to pay taxes on the sale of it, right?

There are quite of a lot of people who believe that because they lived in the home as their main home for two out of five years, they can still utilize the home sell exclusion provisions for the entire sale on their taxes and avoid the capital gains tax. These people usually take the position that they had lived in the home the entire time. I am here to tell you this *could* be WRONG! So, let us review the laws on this issue.

Before taking into account the rental of the home, you must first see if you qualify to exclude all or part of any gain from the sale of your main home.

I.R.C. section 121(a) states gross income shall not include the gain from the sale or exchange of property if, during a five-year period ending on the date of sale or exchange, such property has been owned and used by the taxpayer as the taxpayer's principal residence for periods aggregate two years or more. I.R.C. 121(b)(2) States the property exclusion is $250,000 filing single and $500,000 married file joint for 2022.

What this means is you must meet the ownership and use tests to qualify for this gain exclusion *ending on the date of the sale*. You must have:

- Owned the home for at least two years (the ownership test).
- And lived in the home as your main home for at least two years (the use test).

A vacation home you used that was not your principal residence for at least two years does not qualify for the home exemption.

Be aware that the rental of your home is a sale of a rental asset and might have to be calculated as a rental asset sale. If you are renting the home on the date of the sale, the home may also not qualify for this exclusion.

Under I.R.C. 121(b)(3) the residence will not qualify for the primary residence exclusion if the taxpayer, during a two-year period ending on the date of such sale or exchange, sold another residence and applied the primary residence exclusion to the previous sale.

The exclusion will not apply to the gain from the sale or exchange of property allocated to periods the home was not used as a primary residence by the taxpayer or the taxpayers' spouse. The period the property was not used as the taxpayers' primary residence it considered nonqualified use periods. Nonqualifying use periods include periods of time the residence was being used as a rental.

The gain from the sale or exchange of the property must be allocated between the time the home was rented out and the time the taxpayer or the taxpayers spouse used the property as their main residence.

If you are renting out only a portion of the home when you sell the home, such as using a spare bedroom as a rented room or Airbnb, and you have taken depreciation on the rented portion, you will need to deduct the depreciation allowed or allowable from the cost basis of the home before calculating the home sell exclusion.

You need to determine whether the rental space still counts as a rental space at the time of the sale. A space that was used for business, (rental space) is considered residence space if ALL the following are true:

- You were not using the space for a business purpose or as a rental at the time you sold the property.

- You did not earn any business or rental income from the space in the year you sold your home.

- You used the space as residence space for two years out of the five years leading up to the sale.

Q: If I sell my rental property and purchase a new property within the same year, I do not have to pay taxes on the sale of the rental property I sold, right?

This is also a very popular question among taxpayers that have owned rental properties before the new tax laws came into effect.

This also was true until the Taxpayer Relief Act of 1997 and is no longer true today.

The sale of the old residential or commercial rental sold is a taxable transaction and might need to be reported on your return as a long-term (if held longer than 1 year), short-term (if held for less than 1 year), capital gain or as ordinary income.

Other factors that may determine your taxable transaction amount include things like the amount you originally paid for the rental property you are selling, the type of type of property you sold, (residential rental, commercial rental, etc.), and the amount of depreciation you have taken in on the older rental property including depreciation taken in the year of sale. This is similar to the sale of equipment, except you cannot use bonus depreciation or I.R.C. section 179 depreciation to offset the gain you will realize on the sale of the old residential or commercial rental property you sold or exchanged.

One additional option you have for sell of rental property is using a Like Kind of Exchange (known also as I.R.C. section 1031 to replace the older residential or commercial rental property. Of course, there are pros and cons to this as well.

I.R.C. section 1031 rules also do not apply if the relinquished property is disqualified property. Disqualified property means property that is not held for productive use in a trade or business or held as investment property, (i.e., do not apply to an exchange of one kind or class of property for property of a different kind or class). In other words, you cannot use I.R.C. section 1031 Like Kind of Exchange rules to replace a residential rental property used to produce rental income for a boat or a small airplane you use to take friends vacationing. The boat or airplane are not in the same class as a residential rental property and the boat or small airplane is not business use property.

The Tax Cuts and Jobs Act of 2017 preserved like-kind exchange treatment for residential and commercial real property but eliminated it for personal property. Bottom Line, like-kind exchange treatment is still alive and well for residential and commercial real property, but it is gone for personal property.

Q: If I own a rental and I use all the money I receive in rental income to pay the mortgage, I broke even, so I don't have a tax liability on the rental income, right?

This is an absolute wrong! Part of your mortgage payment on your rental house includes the principal payment for the house. That portion of your mortgage payment is not deductible on the current year taxes. You recover the cost of the rental building through depreciation and recover the cost of the land when the property is sold. Deducting the full amount of the mortgage payment would be considered "double dipping" on your tax return.

The deductions you might be allowed when renting property to offset rental income include most of your operational expenses you pay for maintaining, defending, and managing your rental during the rental period. Deduction also include depreciation on the cost of furniture you included in the property rental, depreciation on the cost of appliances you included in the rental property, as well as depreciation on the cost of the rental building portion you paid for the property.

The depreciation you take is the way you recapture the expenses for the purchase price of the building, the improvements you make, and the appliances you included with the rental property. The depreciation on the cost of the building you are renting can be expensed over 27.5 years for residential property or 39 for commercial rental property. It may not seem as though you are not expensing the cost you paid for the rental property, but depreciation is the way you expense it over the tax life of the rental building.

Q: Can I deduct my rental house if my brother or my adult child is living there paying little to no rent?

I.R.C. section 280A(a) states that an individual or an S Corporation will not be allowed to take taxable deductions for a dwelling unit that is used by the taxpayer for personal use purposes during the taxable year except as otherwise provided under I.R.C. Personal use includes renting below fair market value to family, friends, etc. Therefore, if you are renting to a family member it is considered personal use of the rental if it is not rented at fair market value. Family includes only your spouse, brothers and sisters, half-brothers and half-sisters, ancestors (parents, grandparents, etc.), and lineal descendants (children, grandchildren, etc.).

Fair market value is the price of your property that an unrelated person would be willing to pay to rent the property. The rent you charge to a related person is not a fair rental price if it is substantially less than the rents charged for other properties that are similar to your property in your area, allowing for the facts and circumstances of each property. It can also be considered personal use if you are renting to a friend for less than fair market value.

I had a client that rented out a home for just under three years. In the middle of the third year, she allowed her daughter to move in and pay rent at less than market value. Few landlords consider the impacts of helping family when reporting it on their taxes. However, it's important to consider this, because not only could she no longer deduct all of the rental expenses, but the rental expenses in the third year had to be allocated between rental use, (the period of time regular tenants had been renting the house), and personal use, (the period of time her daughter had been renting the house). Once she rented to her daughter for very little rent, she lost deductions for property taxes, depreciation, repairs, improvements, etc.

If the property is considered personal use property, as in renting it below fair market value to a relative or a friend for more than 14 days and more than 10% of the days of rental use, you are considered to be using it as a personal residence. If you have a net loss, you may not be able to deduct the rental expenses. The expenses are not deductible as rental expenses for the period of time it is considered personal use property.

By the standards of I.R.C. 280A(d)(3), if you rented the residence out to a relative or friend for fair market rental value, you would be allowed to treat the rental income and expenses as though you had no relationship to the tenants, as long as the tenants do not have a financial interest or ownership in the property.

Q: If my adult child's boy/girlfriend lives with me; can I claim them on my taxes?

According to I.R.C. section 152(a), a dependent is (1) a qualifying child, or (2) a qualifying relative. I.R.C. section 152(c)(1) defines a qualifying child as (A) a person who has a relationship to the taxpayer such as a child, a foster child, or a relative, (B) who resides in the same place as the taxpayer for more than half the year, (C) who has not attained the age of 19 at the end of the calendar year, (D) who has not paid over one-half the their own support for over one-half of the calendar year, and who has not filed a joint tax return with a spouse for the taxable year. So, if your adult child is not 19 years of age by the end of the calendar year or is a student under 24 years of age by the end of the calendar year and meets all the other requirements, then you should be able to claim them as a dependent child. On the other hand, under I.R.C. 152(d)(1), your adult child could be a qualifying relative if (A) they do not meet the age requirement of a qualifying child; (B) their gross income is less than their tax exemption amount for the calendar year; (C) you provide over one-half of their support for the calendar year; and (D) they are not a qualifying child of you or another taxpayer for the calendar year. To be a qualifying relative under the standards of I.R.C. 152(d)(2) the person must be (A) a child or descendant of a child; (B) a brother, sister, stepbrother, or stepsister; (C) a father, mother, or ancestor of either; (D) a stepfather or stepmother; (E) a nephew or niece of the taxpayer; (F) an uncle or aunt of the taxpayer; (G) a son-in-law, daughter-in-law, father-in-law, mother-in-law, brother-in-law, or sister-in-law; or (H) an individual who has the same residence, (is a member of the taxpayers household), of the taxpayer during the calendar year.

Given these circumstances, if your child and their boy/girlfriend meet these requirements you might be able to claim them as a qualifying relative on your tax return.

An example of this might be a child living with you who is attending college and then turns 25 years old in the middle of the year. In this circumstance, your child would no longer qualify as your qualifying child, but might qualify as your qualifying relative if your child and you meet all the other requirements.

This might an important area for those of you who have children that have graduated college and cannot find a job. Or maybe you just have a relative that sits on your couch all day and you do not have the heart to kick them out.

A foster child who is placed with you by an authorized placement agency, by judgment, or other order of any court of competent jurisdiction who has lived with you more than half the year can be your qualifying child for the purpose of the member of household test if you paid for over one-half of their support for the year and the natural parents of the child do not file a tax return and claim the child.

I ran across the situation a couple of years ago. The foster child's natural parents filed a tax return so they could claim the child. Even though the child had lived with the foster parents for more than half the year, and the foster parents provided over half the child's support for the year. Because the child's natural parents claimed the child, the foster parent was not allowed to claim the child as a dependent.

However, I.R.C. section 152(b)(3) specifically disqualifies a citizen or a national of the United States unless the individual is a recognized resident of the United States.

To simplify the rules on this issue a bit, there are four tests that must be met for the qualifying relative rules. These four tests are:

Child is not your Qualifying Child Test

Your child is not considered your qualifying relative if the child is your qualifying dependent child or is the qualifying dependent child of any other taxpayer.

A qualifying relative can be any age even if the relative is your son, your stepson, your grandchild, etc.

Example: Your friend who lives with you and is supported by you is not required to file a tax return because your friend did not have enough gross income to be required to file a tax return. You supported your unrelated friend and her 3-year-old child, and they both lived with you all year in your home. Your friend had only $2,500 gross income for the year, and she is not required to file a 2021 tax return. Both your friend and her child are your qualifying relatives if you paid for over half their support for the year.

Member of Household or Relationship Test

To be a member of the household or to meet the relationship test, the person must live with you all year as a member of your household.

The person does not have to live with you all year and is still considered to have lived with you as a member of your household during periods of time when that person is temporarily absent due to such things as illness, education, business, vacation, military service, or detention in a juvenile facility. The membership of household test may also be satisfied if the person is placed in a nursing home for an indefinite period of time in order to receive constant medical care. This is one example of why a person would not necessarily live with you all year but can still be considered a member of your household.

Example: You and your wife began supporting your wife's father in 2018. He lives in an adult care facility. Your wife died in 2021. Even though your wife passed away in 2021, your father-in-law continues to meet the membership of household test, even if he does not live with you. You can claim him as a qualifying relative if all other tests are met, including the gross income test and support test.

I should note; if at any time during the year the person was your spouse, that person cannot be your qualifying relative.

Gross Income Test

The dependent's gross income cannot exceed the amount which would require the dependent to file a tax return, other than to receive a tax refund, not claiming themselves a dependent.

In calculating the dependents gross income for the year, per I.R.C. section 61(a), gross income is all income from whatever source, such as but not limited to, compensation for services, business income, interest, etc. Gross income must also include income from discharged debts, such as discharged credit card debt. You cannot deduct expenses for the dependents' rental expenses such as taxes, repairs, or other expenses to determine the gross income from any rental property for the gross income test. Gross income also includes all taxable unemployment compensation received, all taxable social security benefits received, and certain amounts received for scholarship and fellowship grants.

Support Test

For a person to be considered a qualifying relative, you must usually provide over one-half of a person's total support during the calendar year. The easiest way to figure out if you have provided more than one-half of a person's total support is by comparing the amount you contributed to that person's support with the entire amount of support that person received from all sources. However, the person's own money is not considered support unless it is actually spent their money for their support.

You can take support items into consideration when calculating the financial support your provided. Support includes things like the cost of lodging where you and the other person lives, the cost of food, the cost of utilities, the cost of the other persons transportation, the cost of repairs of the home where you both live, the costs of home maintenance, the cost of home insurance, and the cost of real estate taxes of the home where both of you live.

Q: What kind of charitable deductions can I take, and can I deduct the time I donated to a charitable organization? Even if I donate my time in an activity I do professionally?

I.R.C. section 170(a)(1) allows as a deduction most charitable contribution payments made within the taxable year to a qualified charitable organization. A charitable contribution shall be allowable as a deduction, but only if verified under regulations prescribed by the Secretary. With subsection (c), special limitations with respect to contributions of certain capital gains property apply. However, there are other restrictions and limitations due to the *"only if verified under regulations prescribed by the Secretary of Treasury"* language.

Some of the limitations included in I.R.C. section 170(b) includes charitable donation deduction percentage limitations for individuals. I.R.C. section 17(b)(1)(A) confine charitable donations to churches, convention of churches, or association of churches to 60 percent or less in cash donations of the taxpayer's adjusted gross income without regard to the taxpayer's net operating loss carryback to the taxable year. I.R.C. section 170(b)(1)(G) increased the limitation from 50 percent to 60 percent and is available to taxpayers from 2018 to 2025. After 2025 the limit may be reduced to the original 50 percent limitation as prescribed by statute.

I.R.C. section 170(b)(1)(B) further confines other charitable contributions, that are not described as a church, convention of churches, or association of churches, to the lesser of 30 percent of the taxpayers adjusted gross income or 60 percent for cash donations of the taxpayer's adjusted gross income for the taxable year over the amount of charitable contributions to church or church organizations.

Example: Your adjusted gross income for the year is $100,000. If you itemize your deductions, you contribute $70,000 total for the year to different churches and other qualified organizations. Of the $70,000 in donations, $50,000 was to churches. You will be allowed a deduction of $10,000 for the year to other organizations because the maximum charitable donations you are allowed is limited to $60,000 (or 60 percent of your adjusted gross income for the year of 2021). You may be allowed to carry over the remaining $10,000 of donations to the following next five years until the additional charitable contribution has been deducted or the carryover period has expired.

If you are not itemizing deductions (filing a schedule A), you can still deduct $600 cash donations if married filing joint and $300 cash donations if you are filing single in 2021. This amount is a graduated rate but has not been updated for 2022 yet.

I caution you by saying if you are not itemizing deduction for federal tax purposes, you could be among the taxpayers that commonly misunderstand this deduction. Some taxpayers seem to be under the disillusion that a $600 charitable donation reduces their taxes by $600. That is not the way charitable donations work. The $600 charitable donation reduces your *taxable income* by $600. It does not reduce your *tax liability* by $600. The charitable donation is deducted from your *taxable income before* your tax is calculated.

Example: Taxpayer has adjusted gross income of $60,000.00. Taxpayer files single and itemizes deductions as follows:

$3060.00 State Taxes Paid

$1500.00 Property Taxes Paid

$7500.00 Mortgage Interest Paid

<u>$1000.00</u> Charitable Cash donation Paid

$13,060.00 Itemized Deductions

With no other adjustments to income, the taxpayer has $46,940.00 Taxable Income.

You can see from the example that charitable donations do reduce your taxes, but not as much as you might think, unless you are donating quite a bit of money or property and the standard deduction is lower than your itemized deductions for federal tax purposes.

I.R.C. section 170(a)(1) allows charitable donations *"only if verified under regulations prescribed by the Secretary,"* and the secretary specifically states the value of your time is not considered a charitable donation, you are not allowed to deduct the value of your time regardless of your occupation.

When you are providing services for free that you typically charge others for, you would think it only makes sense that you could take the time you donated as a charitable donation. But could you imagine how badly this could be abused if it were allowed? That is not the way tax code is written and is also one of the many reasons this is simply a big NO.

However, you can count the costs of materials and supplies you paid for that were used in the time you donated as a deduction such as boxes you purchased to transport items for donation. You may also be able to write off the mileage of your personal vehicle used to donate your time and services to the charitable organization.

Example: You are a plumber, and you volunteer your time to work on a special project for a not-for-profit group. You purchased plumbing supplies for the project. You can deduct the plumbing supplies as a charitable donation, but your time in not allowed in the deduction.

This can be true as long as the organization is recognized as a legitimate charitable organization by the IRS. You can find a list of qualified organizations for the purpose of tax exempt status on-line by searching https://www.irs.gov/charities-non-profits/tax-exempt-organization-search and follow the links of the search tool if you are uncertain if an organization qualifies as a qualified organization. You can also search IRS Pub 78 (data) and find most information about an organization. I repeat this numerous times because not all organizations qualify your donation for a charitable deduction.

With sports-oriented nonprofits it can be difficult to know how to categorize your charitable deduction. Purely recreational sports, such as church softball leagues, are usually tagged as I.R.C. section 501(c)(7) social or recreational groups that even though tax-exempt, are not charitable donations for tax purposes. Also, youth-only sports groups, such as Little League baseball, can qualify for I.R.C. section 501(c)(3) status, but they are considered educational in nature-not charitable donations for tax deductions that fit within this type of charitable donations. *Professional* athletic competitions also are not recognized as a non-profit group. They are considered a commercial activity.

Clear examples of I.R.C. section 501(c)(3) are amateur sports groups. These groups are those that fall into competitions groups like the Olympic Games. Included in this category are groups that demonstrate the difference between truly amateur athletics and your local YMCA swim club-type groups.

In order to take a tax deduction for mileage, the charitable organization must be a tax-exempt, I.R.C. section 501(c)(3) organization. A non-profit must exist for one or more exclusively charitable purposes. *Charitable purpose* means it exists for the benefit of religious groups, federal and state agencies as long as the contributions are solely for public purposes. Included with this group are domestic fraternal organizations, orders and associations that is used solely for the purpose of scientific, literary, educational, and prevention of animal cruelty or child abuse, testing for public safety, educational, and fostering of national or international amateur sports.

With most gifts, tax law requires you to obtain an appraisal from a qualified appraiser if you are gifting property with a fair market value over $5,000 to a charitable organization. A qualified appraisal is only required for donations of vehicles.

Q: What is the difference between tax deductions and tax credits?

To understand why charitable donations do not affect your taxes the way you might like to think they do, you have to understand the difference between tax deductions and tax credits.

Qualified charitable donations are a good example of a tax deduction for those that itemize their taxes. Other types of tax deductions that are common when you itemize your deductions are property taxes, state taxes paid, medical deductions, and mortgage interest deductions. If you do not itemize deductions on your tax return, you have the standard deduction. These typical tax deductions reduce your taxable income.

Tax credits reduce your tax liability dollar for dollar, sometimes to zero. Tax credits reduce the amount of taxes you have to pay after calculating your adjusted gross income. Some of the most common tax credits are the child tax credit, the child and dependent care credit, the earned income tax credit, the educational credits, and the credit for other dependents. Some of these credits, such as the earned income credit and the educational credit, can result in a tax refund after your tax liability has been reduced to zero.

Example: Your adjusted gross income is $65,000 and you take the standard deduction, which is $12,950 for filing single for the tax year 2022. Your taxable income would be $52,050.00 for the year. If you had no tax credits, your taxes would be $7,068.00 for the year. If you also had an education credit in the amount of $2,500.00, your taxes would be $4,568.00 for the year because most tax credits reduce your tax liability, whereas tax deductions reduce your taxable gross income.

As you can see, tax credits are very advantageous, but most tax credits do come with income limitation caps. Most, if not all, credits are at reduced or eliminated as your adjusted gross income reaches the income limitation caps.

Q: What will my relative have to pay in tax if I gift them money?

Strangely enough, I do get the question of how much a person receiving a gift will have to pay in taxes if the taxpayer gifts the other person money. This question usually comes from people wanting to pay off the mortgage of their son or daughter's house or wanting to pay some debt of their unmarried significant other.

I cannot emphasize enough: it is not the person receiving the gift that will be responsible for any tax liability when the gift is given to them. It is the person giving the gift that may be responsible for the gift taxes.

I.R.C. section 102(a) clearly states gross income does not include the value of property acquired by gift, bequest, device, or inheritance. The donor may be subject to a gift tax for gifts valued over the current annual exemption amount if the total gifts the donor has given in their lifetime exceeds the 2022 federal gift limitation of $12.6 million. The $12.6 million lifetime limitation could be subject to change by Congress. Taxpayers have also asked me how much they can deduct on their own tax return if they give a gift to their son, daughter or significant other, such as paying off another person's debt.

By IRS standards, to be considered a gift (charitable or otherwise), the person receiving the gift must have unfettered right, use, and access to the money or property. So, things like free rent are not considered a gift for charitable, or any other gift tax purpose.

There are some exceptions to gift laws. Generally, the following gifts are not subject to gift tax and do not require you to file a form 709 gift tax return:

1) Gifts that are less than the annual exclusion for the calendar year. The annual exclusion is the limit that you are allowed to gift and avoid the tax reporting requirements. For 2022 the annual exclusion is $16,000.

2) Tuition or medical expenses you pay for someone else (the educational and medical exclusions).

3) Gifts to your spouse.

4) Gifts to a political organization.

Aside from the exceptions listed above, the donor giving the gift must know the fair market value and your adjusted basis in the gift on the date you give the gift. Your adjusted basis is generally your cost plus improvements, less depreciation allowed or allowable, amortization, or depletion.

You will not be required to pay tax on the gift or file a form 709 Gift Tax Return if the gift's fair market value you are giving does not exceed an annual value of $16,000 (2022 annual exclusion per person and per donor).

You and your spouse qualify for the annual exclusion separately. So, you can both give an annual gift of $16,000 in 2022 per gift receiver. A couple married filing joint can jointly give annual gifts of $32,000.00, even if the gift comes from the same checking account or if both your names are on the property you are giving.

If you are a citizen or resident of the United States, you must file a gift tax return (whether or not any tax is due) in the following situation:

> If you gave gifts to someone in 2022 totaling more than $16,000. Even though each spouse is allowed an annual gift exclusion in 2022 of $16,000 because spouses may not file a joint gift tax return even if the gift is jointly owned. Each individual is responsible for his or her own Form 709 Gift Tax Return.

Example: You and your spouse jointly own a boat with a fair market value of $40,000. You can both give the boat to your son. Each of you would file a form 709 Gift Tax Return. You would claim one-half of the fair market value of the boat ($20,000) on your separate 709 Gift Tax Return and your spouse would claim the other one-half ($20,000) on their separate 709 Gift Tax Return.

Future interest gifts are not subject to the $16,000 2022 annual exclusion and you must file Form 709 even if the gift was under $16,000. A gift is considered a future interest if the person receiving the gift does not have the rights to the use, possess, and enjoy the property or income from the property currently. Some examples of future interests might include interests in a trust, or an estate.

Just to be clear, a gift is considered a present interest if that gift is available for current use, enjoyment, and right of use. I.R.C. section 2503(c)(1) specifically states no part of a gift to an individual who is not currently age 21 years or younger on the date of the transfer of the gift shall be considered a gift of a future interest in property for purposes of the annual exclusion, if the property and the income may be used by or for the benefit of that person before that person reaches the age of 21.

The gift tax applies not only to the free transfer of any kind of money or property, but as per I.R.C. section 2512(b), the gift tax also applies to sales or exchanges for less than full fair market value. This occurs where value of the property received is less than the fair market value of the property sold or exchanged. This does not include property sold in the ordinary course of business, such as discounts on products. The amount of the gifts given less than the full amount of value is to be calculated as part of the donor's annual gift exclusion as well as the donor's lifetime gift limitations for the purpose gift taxes.

This is another part of the Internal Revenue Code that people tend to be unaware of. Even if you transfer property for less than fair market value, it can be considered a gift and may require a Form 709 Gift Tax Return.

I have a client that delt with this situation in 2021. She had sold her rental house to her son for $285,000 but the fair-market value of the house was $350,000. She had to file a gift tax return on the $65,000 reduction in the sale price.

Q: Can I deduct my travels for work if I work out of town for my employer?

Simply said, NO, not at this time. The employee business expense deductions have been suspended until 01/01/2026. The suspension of this deduction went into effect with the 2017 Tax Cut and Jobs Act. It might be put back into play after 2025 when the 2017 Tax Cut and Jobs Act expires. But until then, the best you can do is negotiate with your employer to create an employee reimbursement plan for travel expenses, hotel expenses, meals while traveling for your employer, and any other expenses you may incur while traveling for your employers' benefit that complies with IRS regulations. Your employer can write off the reimbursement to you as a business expense if done correctly. But you are not allowed to deduct any employee business expenses at this time.

Q: If my employer requires me to wear outfits or professional clothing for my business, I can deduct the cost of the clothing I purchased, right?

Sorry to say, that is also NO. Deducting <u>any</u> clothing as a W-2 employee is no longer allowed, including safety clothing and uniforms, until the Tax Cut and Jobs Act of 2017 expires. Prior to the 2017 Tax Cut and Jobs Act, a taxpayer that itemized deductions on schedule A could deduct clothing items such as safety clothing and unforms not provided by your employer on form 2106--Employee Business Expenses. These expenses were calculated for amounts totally over 2% of the taxpayer's adjusted gross income. These deductions were suspended, at least until 01/01/2026. Congress may modify this suspension before that time. But for now, these types of deductions are no longer allowed.

Q: I prepared my own taxes by using a free (or low cost) online tax software. I followed the directions exactly and answered all questions, but the IRS says I owe more in taxes because of an error. Isn't the tax software company liable for some or all of the taxes, penalties, or interest since it was their software?

The quick answer to this is NO! In fact, you are signing that tax return stating that it is true and accurate to the best of your knowledge under penalty of perjury. Ultimately, you are responsible to pay the correct amount of taxes.

Most tax software has a disclaimer in the Terms and Conditions stating they are not offering legal advice or any other advice to customers. This disclaimer usually contains language holding them harmless of any responsibility if the tax return is done incorrectly. The language is in the Terms and Conditions usually require you to agree to these terms prior to using the software. Many of these tax software companies offer, at an additional cost, "Peace of Mind Insurance" that is intended to assist taxpayers in cases where there are errors on the tax returns. Omissions you do not report on the tax return are generally not covered in the Peace of Mind insurance you purchase.

Free (or low cost) on-line tax software is suitable for people who have a simple tax return and have income that is $73,000 or less a year. Simple tax returns for people who only have one or two W-2's, have no other income, have no children to claim as dependents, only lived in one state for the entire year, and who do not need to itemize their mortgage interest and property taxes, typically need not worry about using free (or low cost) on-line tax software. People that fit in this category claim that the programs are simple to use, and they save money by not paying a professional tax preparer.

As of 2019, the IRS has its own free-file option on https://www.irs.e-file.com that is perfect for some people who do not need to file a state return, whose income is under $73,000 and do not itemize deductions. The IRS e-file free program does not prepare state tax returns for free in most cases. This option also comes with a disclaimer stating, the taxpayer or person preparing the tax return should know how to use the IRS form instructions and publications to prepare their tax if needed.

Before 2019, the IRS had entered into an agreement with companies called the Free File Alliance. This agreement allowed these companies an opportunity to provide the link to their company's free tax filing on the IRS Free File website. In return, the IRS agreed not to enter the tax return software and e-file services marketplace.

In 2019, the Treasury Inspector General for Tax Administration performed an audit of the Free File system. The audit indicated that some of the companies partnering with the IRS in the Free File Alliance were making it difficult for users to find the link for the "free tax filing" services within their website. The audit report indicated this was done so that tax return filers would use the paid version of these companies' software. After the audit report was released, the IRS released an addendum to its Free File program. This addendum eliminated the restrictions on the IRS and enabled the IRS to venture into their own free filing software. However, all the free filing software has its own pros and cons.

If you have a simple return and you *do* need to file a state return, Turbo Tax, H&R Block, Tax Slayer, and a few others offer free or (or low cost) on-line federal tax return preparation software. These companies do sometimes offer the state tax return preparation software for an additional fee.

Turbo Tax has pricing that allows you to file your simple federal form 1040 tax return for free. But if you need live, online support from them, there is a charge. Turbo Tax also charges you if your tax return filing requires more than filing just the easy federal form 1040. H&R Block offers free federal tax return filing, but they charge for state tax filing. H&R Block also charges for live on-line support. Tax Slayer charges for state tax filing, and they only offer live on-line support if you purchase one of their pricier packages. These are just a few of the companies that offer free (or low cost) on-line tax preparation software with "Peace of Mind Insurance" for an additional cost if you want additional reassurance that you prepared your return properly.

For people who fall under the "more complicated tax returns," such as those who have lived in more than one state in the year, have other sources of income, who have dependents to claim, etc., I recommend the use of a professional tax preparer if you want to be on the safer side. Tax law have become increasingly complicated and difficult to master for the average taxpayer. Therefore most, but not all, people in the professional tax advising and tax preparation industry must spend several hours and quite a bit of money every year to become well-versed on the current tax laws and regulations. If you complain about the cost of a tax professional preparing your tax return, you should ask yourself how often you are able to get free legal advice from a professional with no strings attached?

Q: Once a taxpayer reaches a certain age, they no longer have to file taxes, right?

The answer to that question is **That depends**. If your only source of income is social security, a small amount of interest income, a small amount of dividend income, or non-taxable disability and your total adjusted gross income does exceed your standard deduction for the year you will most likely not be required to file a tax return.

For 2022, that income limit is $14,350 for an individual and $27,300 for a married couple filing jointly if one spouse is over 65 and an additional $1,400 if both spouses are over 65 years of age.

On the other hand, if you have self-employment income, stocks, bonds, an IRA, or other taxable sources of income, you will most likely be required to prepare a tax return at any age. I.R.C. section 6012(1)(A)(i) clearly states every individual having taxable gross income for the year which equals or exceeds their exemption amount for their filing status, and has taxable gross income which equals or exceeds the individual's, exemption amount, plus additional standard deduction allowances for the taxable year, shall file a tax return

Per I.R.C. section 691(a)(1), your representative, or your estate administrator may even be required to file a tax return after you are deceased. That is right, if you had taxable gross income in the year of your death, or from a prior period for which a tax return has not been filed, or you left behind any assets to be inherited, a final tax return may need to be filed, regardless of not having other sources of income during your lifetime and regardless of your age at the time of your death.

Q: If the IRS owes me a refund, I can wait three years to file my tax return, right?

This is not recommended. How do you know if you are getting a refund unless you fill out the tax return forms? You should not rely upon your best guess.

You need to be aware I.R.C. section 6511(a) asserts the period of time on claiming a credit or a refund for an overpayment of tax in which a tax return is required to be filed, the taxpayer shall claim the credit or refund of an overpayment within three years from the time the tax return was filed or two years from the time the tax was paid, whichever of such periods expires later, or if no return was filed by the taxpayer, within two years from the time the tax was paid.

So, if you miss the two-year deadline from the date the taxes were paid or three-year deadline from the date the tax return was filed by even one day, you will not receive a tax refund. If you do file within the time limit allowed the tax refund you expect to receive will most likely take 3-9 months to receive as well.

I just conducted a collection due process hearing for a client that had not filed her taxes for the prior 10 years. The IRS file an SFR on the unfiled years based on information sent to them from 3rd-parties. The IRS had calculated her tax liability to be just over $76,000. I filed all 10 years for her.

Because 2011-2018 where out of statue for claiming a refund, she lost over $7,900 in refunds. Fortunately, she ended up owing around $11,485 by the time we filed her tax returns. But the $7,900 would have gone a long way in reducing the final tax liability had she filed her taxes within the 3-year period.

The prior year's tax returns are processed at the back of the line as they take more time to be processed. Whereas if you had electronically filed your tax return by the due date or the due date of your extension, you most likely would have received your refund 2-8 weeks after the tax return was filed.

In addition to all of these issues you might face by waiting to file your tax return, if you unexpectedly owe even the smallest amount of taxes you will most likely be charged late payment penalties, late filing penalties, interest, and could also be charges other penalties and interest depending upon your circumstances.

Additionally, if you neglect to file your taxes in a timely manner, the IRS can file what is called a Substitute For Return (SFR) any time after the due date or extension due date of the return. When the IRS files a Substitute For Return (SFR) for taxpayers, they typically only include information they have received from third party reporters.

What that means for the taxpayer is they will only give you deductions and credits for things that were reported to them, such as federal tax withholding from your W-2, mortgage interest deductions, or federal tax withholding from your 1099-R (Distributions from Pension, Annuities, Retirement Form). The IRS does not give you deductions for things like dependency claims, property taxes, charitable contributions, state tax withholding, or investment interest deductions. The IRS also does not give you credits such as child tax credits, educational credits, earned income credits and retirement savings credits.

For example, when calculating your taxable gain on any stock and bond sales that have been reported to them, they usually do not subtract your basis (i.e., your cost) from the gain of these stock and bond sales.

Example: Betty did not file her tax return for 2019. She sold her ABC stock in 2019 and received gross proceeds of $87,000. Her basis (cost) in the stock of $76,500 was not reported to the IRS. In 2020, Betty received a letter from the IRS stating she owed the IRS $13,050 for the sales of her stock in ABC. After receiving the letter, Betty had her 2019 taxes filed and her actual taxes owed was $1,575 plus penalties and interest that have been accumulating for over a year. Betty could have avoided this headache by filing her tax return when it was due and most likely would have saved the additional money she had to pay in penalties and interest.

I helped a client with a similar situation a couple of years ago. In this client's situation, she had filed her own tax return and did not report her stock sales at all. She believed she had a loss on the sale of the stock, but she did not know how to report the loss. So, she did not report the stock sale on her original return. She received a letter from the IRS stating she owned an additional $3,800.00 for underreported income. The investment company handling her stock reported the sale of the stock to the IRS, but they did not report what she had paid for the stock to the IRS. I amended the tax return reporting her basis (cost) in the stock to the IRS. Once this transaction was properly reported to the IRS, she did in fact have a capital loss and she received a tax refund.

I also want to point out that tax season is the busiest time of the year for most people in the professional tax preparation industry. Most people in the tax preparation industry will only put a prior's year tax returns at the front of the line if a tax refund is expected and the three-year statute of limitation to receive the refund is too close for comfort. Tax professionals may also immediately address the tax return if the client has received a demand letter from the IRS indicating a deadline to respond. When dealing with the IRS and State Taxing Authorities, all clients' tax concerns are important. But when tax professionals are in tax season, their main focus is on getting current year tax returns filed on time.

Think of it this way: if you are the business owner of an auto repair shop, do you prioritize your customers that come in for oil changes every six months first or do you let their vehicle sit while you rebuild an engine for a customer that just came into your shop for the first time? The auto repair shop has no idea how long the engine rebuild will take until the repair technician diagnoses the vehicle. It is the same way with tax clients that you are just seeing for the first time that need IRS representation issues addressed. You have no idea how long the new client issues will take, and it is your busiest time of the year. You must address any representation deadlines while also meeting the regular filing deadlines of your clients.

Q: How long do I have to keep tax records and tax returns?

The mindful taxpayer asks the question of how long they should keep tax return records and tax receipts. Although three years is the standard answer they will receive when asking a tax professional, the answer should be based on personal knowledge of the taxpayer, the taxpayers return in question, and the type of tax return.

The simple answer is found in I.R.C. section 6501(a), which states the amount of any tax imposed shall be assessed within three years after the return was filed or the due date the tax return was due to be filed. I.R.C. section 6501(b)(1) describes the individual tax return filing due date as April 15th of the following calendar year. This is true even if the return was filed earlier. Because the IRS has three years to assess or audit a tax return after it is filed, most tax professionals will advise taxpayers to keep tax return documents and tax returns for three years.

The assessment statutory limitation does come with exceptions. I.R.C. section 6501(c) states this limitation for tax assessment does not apply in cases where there is a false or fraudulent tax return filed, where there is an attempt to evade taxes, and where there is no tax return filed by the taxpayer.

What this means is no statute of limitation exists until the taxpayer files the tax return for the year and no statute of limitation exists when the taxpayer files a false or fraudulent tax return. There is also no statute of limitation exists when the taxpayer intentionally evades taxes. If the IRS files a SFR (Substitute For Return), the statute of limitations does not start until the taxpayer files their own tax return.

The statute of limitations as prescribed by the I.R.C. sets the statute of limitations in which the IRS can assess if a filed tax return has errors. These statutes cover errors such as mathematical errors, unreported income errors, and tax credit errors. The statutes do not restrict the IRS from auditing tax returns older than three years old that are fraudulent tax returns or have fraudulent unreported income or fraudulent tax credit claims.

I suggest the tax professional have personal knowledge of the taxpayer and the tax returns of that taxpayer because if the tax return has adjustments and deductions that extend beyond the prior three years, the records that support those adjustments and deductions should be kept three years after the adjustment or deduction was last reflected on the tax return.

Example: Taxpayer Joe files his tax return married filing joint and sold stock in which he had a capital loss of $15,000 on his 2020 tax return. Over the next five years Joe had no other capital gains or losses. Joe can deduct $3,000 per year on his tax return for the next five years. Because Joe can deduct $3,000 per year on his tax return for tax years 2020 through 2025, Joe should keep tax records and documents that support the $15,000 capital loss carry until 2029, three years from the last tax return filing year he could claim the capital loss carryover.

One of my clients faced large stock market losses in 2008. He and his wife were planning to retire. So, when his stock sharply dropped, he panicked and sold his stock at a loss of $37,000. Because all of his stock sales were losses, he could only deduct $3,000 in 2008 against his regular income. I explained to him that he would need to keep proof of his loss until 2015 because he would be deducting $3,000 a year against his income from 2008 through 2012 but he could be audited on his 2012 loss deduction until 2015.

This is just an example of what type of records I believe should be kept longer than three years. There are many other types of records that could affect tax returns in future years, such as business loss carryovers that can be carried over into future years where tax return records should be kept longer.

Q: What is the difference between Tax Fraud, Tax Evasion, and Tax Avoidance?

Tax fraud by the standards of I.R.C section 7206(1) is committed by any person who willfully files a tax return under false pretenses that person knows to be untrue. Fraud also includes a person who makes a statement to the IRS, or on any tax document and declares that it is made under the penalties of perjury, which that person does not believe to be true and correct as to every material matter. This is the statement every taxpayer declares every year when filing their tax return.

In other words, if you claim you spent $20,000 on a remodel for your rental home, when you in fact spent that money on your personal residence, that would be considered fraud. Remember, you signed that tax return under penalty of perjury that it is true and accurate to the best of your knowledge.

Tax fraud can also be committed under I.R.C. section 7206(2) by any person that willfully aids, assists in, or advises in the preparation or presentation of a tax return for others, which is fraudulent or is false as to any material matter. This can be construed as fraud whether or not the fraudulent statement is made with the knowledge or consent of the person authorized or required to present such return, affidavit, claim, or document.

This was the case with Brittany Patterson. She was a tax preparer that actually advertised her clients could "buy dependents" to claim on their tax return. She signed the tax returns she prepared knowing the tax returns were fraudulent. She was charged with fraudulently assisting in the preparation of false tax returns and was sentenced to one year and one day in prison for defrauding the US government.

Tax Evasion as defined by I.R.C. section 7201 is an act in which the taxpayer willfully attempts to evade or defeat any tax imposed by not paying the amount of tax imposed by their own tax return, a SFR filed by the IRS, or tax return amount adjusted by the IRS. . To clarify, tax evasion is committed by any person who willfully attempts to avoid paying taxes imposed.

Tax avoidance as prescribed by the IRS can be fluid in terms. Every individual is expected to voluntarily comply with tax laws to file and when filing their tax return and do it without government interference. Because tax loopholes when unlawfully used can be construed as tax avoidance schemes, taxpayers who unlawfully use these loopholes in a manner inconsistent with tax law can also be considered fraudulent. There are more than a few bad actors out there that claim unlawful tax loopholes are perfectly legal.

When taxpayers use the unlawful tax loopholes or use tax loopholes in a manner inconsistent with tax laws, it does raise flags with the IRS. The IRS can and most likely will go over the tax return with a fine-toothed comb if the tax return is flagged for any purpose. Attempting to use loopholes in an unlawful manner may also have the IRS looking at tax returns filed for other years.

Types of Tax Relief Available to Taxpayers Who Can Not Pay their Tax Liability

Throughout history, Congress has attempted to create a better image of United States tax collection and the IRS and to paint it as fair, balanced, and impartial. The United States' economic depressions and economic recessions have periodically made tax collection efforts difficult. Once a taxpayer gets behind on their taxes, the debt can become exacerbated by penalties and interest constantly accruing, only adding to the issue. If the taxpayer has no means to pay their tax debt, below are some of the other avenues taxpayers can consider to resolve their tax debt with the IRS:

Offer In Compromise: Taxpayers can offer the IRS less than the full tax debt to settle their tax debt. With an Offer In Compromise, the IRS considers the taxpayer's ability to pay the full debt based on the taxpayer's income, expenses, and equity in their assets. The IRS generally approves the Offer In Compromise if the IRS believes the tax debt settlement is the most amount of money they can expect to collect from the taxpayer over a reasonable time period.

Taxpayers must meet certain criteria for an Offer In Compromise to be considered. The taxpayer must have filed all prior year tax returns, made all required estimated tax payments, cannot be in bankruptcy, and must have filed for an extension of time to file on their current year tax return if it has not already been filed.

Taxpayers may find this favorable because it can alleviate tax lien stresses, so the taxpayer does not have to worry about IRS wage and bank garnishments.

While the IRS is considering the taxpayer's Offer In Compromise, the ten-year statute of limitations for collection of taxes is tolled. Which means the time allowed for the IRS to collect the debt is extended.

Installment Agreement: Taxpayers can enter into an installment agreement with the IRS to pay off their tax debt. When taxpayers enter into an installment agreement, the taxpayer must make the tax payments as agreed. Entering to an installment agreement does not guarantee tax liens will be eliminated, but the IRS is more willing to lift tax liens already in place if they believe the taxpayer will honor the installment agreement, pay the tax debt in full and on time.

Bankruptcy: Taxpayers do have an option to file bankruptcy to eliminate their tax debt. Bankruptcy discharge of federal income tax debt has very stringent rules and regulations though. Filing Chapter 13 bankruptcy does stop interest and penalties from accruing. What the taxpayer owes on the date of the bankruptcy filing date is what the taxpayer will owe on the tax debt. Filing Chapter 13 bankruptcy can also force the IRS into an installment agreement that the IRS has already denied as well as lower the payments the IRS refused to agree to originally. Chapter 13 bankruptcy on tax debt can reduce older unsecured penalty claims as well. But with Chapter 13 bankruptcy, the taxpayer will still be obligated to repay the tax debt.

Taxpayers can file Chapter 7 bankruptcy, which will eliminate the tax debt, the penalties, and the interest within 4-6 months. If the taxpayer has financial issues with credit card debt, medical debt, etc., filing Chapter 7 bankruptcy will eliminate all the debt at once as well.

The pros to filing either Chapter 13 or Chapter 7 bankruptcy is of course the elimination of tax debt, penalties, and interest. And if this is the only option the taxpayer has because they cannot qualify for an Offer In Compromise, do not have the financial resources to pay tax debt through an installment agreement or both, it may be the only avenue available to bring tax debt nightmares to an end.

The cons to filing either Chapter 13 or Chapter 7 bankruptcy is the timing to qualify as well as other rules that must be met. The bankruptcy must be filed more than three years after the tax return was due or filed including extensions. The bankruptcy must be filed more than two years after the tax return was actually filed in addition to the three-year rule. The client must pass both tests to begin the process of eliminating federal tax debt in bankruptcy.

In addition to these requirements, the bankruptcy must be filed more than 240 days after the tax was assessed by the IRS. What this means is if the tax return was filed by the due date of the tax return and the IRS later audits the tax return and assesses additional taxes two-and-a-half years later, the taxpayer must wait a full 240 days from the date of the assessment to file bankruptcy.

Another con to filing bankruptcy on tax debt is the only type of tax debt that can be eliminated through bankruptcy is income tax. State taxes may qualify, but payroll taxes that are employee withholding taxes do not.

TAX TIPS AND HINTS:

When preparing tax returns and discussing tax planning with my clients, I put quite a bit of effort into saving my clients money on their tax returns legally. Many taxpayers may find some tax relief from a few of the tax tips and hints in this section. Even though you may not be able to gain tax relief from utilizing all of favorable so-called tax loopholes for individuals, hopefully you will find some of these useful in reducing your tax liability.

As with all tax regulations and laws, there are factors that must be met and circumstances the taxpayer should have to find these tax loopholes of use.

Medical Savings Plans

One of my personal favorite tax savings tips for individual taxpayers is health savings account contributions, (contributions to an HSA-Health Savings Account or MSA-Medical Savings Account). To utilize this tax savings, you must meet the following criteria:

- You cannot be a qualifying dependent of another taxpayer on the other taxpayers' tax return.
- You cannot be enrolled in Medicare (meaning you are generally not 65 years of age or older).
- You are not enrolled in another health insurance plan as well as the qualified highly deductible plan (unless you are in a plan with certain limiting types of coverage).
- You are enrolled in a qualified highly deductible plan.

The many benefits of a Health Savings Plan are that you can participate in the tax savings even if you are enrolled through your employer and you also contribute matching funds to the HSA or MSA.

When using an HSA or MSA to pay for out-of-pocket medical expenses, you do not have to itemize deductions to take advantage of deducting your medical expenses.

The amount you contribute can be deductible up to $3,650 for an individual account with self-coverage or $7,300 for an individual with family coverage per year.

You can deduct up to these amounts without itemizing.

If you are age 55 or older, you can make catch-up contributions of as much as an additional $1,000 per year.

Higher earning taxpayers can participate in the tax savings in the health savings account tax benefits.

When you withdraw the money from the HSA or MSA, the money you withdraw is 100% tax free as long as the money withdrawn is spent on qualified medical expenses. But be warned, if you do not use the money contributed to the HSA or MSA for qualified medical expenses, is included in gross income for the year of the withdraw and is subject to a 20% penalty.

Short-Term 14-Day Rentals

Another way individual taxpayers can make some extra tax-free money and save on their taxes is to rent out a vacation home or guest house, at fair market value, for 14 days or less. If you rent out a vacation home or other residents for 14 days or less, the income you earn from the short-term rental is non-taxable. You cannot deduct the expenses, such as utilities, maintenance, etc., for the time period you rent the residence, but you do not have to include the income either.

Capital Loss Deductions

If a taxpayer has capital losses in excess of capital gains, the taxpayer can only deduct $3,000 of that loss per year to offset ordinary income such as wages or business income. If the taxpayer dies before deducting all of the prior year capital losses, those losses are gone forever. One way to access those capital losses and deduct them in the current tax year is to sell off those assets that have built-in capital gains, recognize the capital gains to use up the capital losses, and repurchase the assets at the current fair market value.

In doing this, the taxpayer uses up their capital losses against the capital gains and the new higher cost basis allows for additional losses in later years. There is no rule that indicates a taxpayer cannot sell their assets, offset the capital gains with capital losses, and immediately repurchase the assets.

Hiring Your Children

As a self-employed person or a partner in a partnership, you have the advantage of hiring your children to work in your business and get tax advantages. The wages you pay to a child under the age of 18 are not subject to Social Security tax, Medicare tax, or federal unemployment tax. In some states the wages are also not subject to state unemployment tax. Your child can earn income up to the standard deduction for a single person and the child will not be subject to federal taxes. For the tax year 2022 that amount is $12,950 for federal tax purposes. You will also need to take into consideration the laws are in the state you live in regarding to this deduction. If your state standard deduction is less than the federal amount, some of the wages you pay to your child may be subject to state taxes.

The child can contribute that money to a Roth IRA and enjoy the benefit of withdrawing the money distributed to a Roth IRA tax-free and penalty-free at any time if the child contributes the wages the child earned from you. The child can also invest those wages in a college savings account.

It is a win-win if the process is done properly. You get to deduct the wages paid to them, and the child is not subject to federal taxes on the wages. However, the child must be actually working for your business, which means you can have them stuffing envelopes, inputting data into a computer, or any other task you hire them to do.

Like any other employee, your child must keep a track of their time working for you in the same manner as other employees you have working for you. You must document hours worked and rate of pay. You must treat the paychecks you pay to your child as you would any other employee, with the exception of withholding federal Social Security tax, federal Medicare tax, federal withholding tax, and paying federal unemployment tax on their wages. So special record-keeping will be required for filing payroll tax reports, but you can save on your taxes if it is done correctly.

CONCLUSION

While doing the research for this book, it was particularly interesting to me the distortion some people have of the United States tax history, the stunning myths people believe, as well as what people will do to try avoiding paying the government taxes. Most of the questions covered are questions from my own clients over the years.

The materials in this book are comprised from my own years of experience in the tax preparation industry, continuing education, and knowledge I have obtained throughout the years, as well as information I have obtained both online and in printed materials.

I found several online sources to portray both the history of taxation and the factual substance of tax laws. But the most helpful resource was the National Archives tax records and the years of education I have obtained from professional instruction. It is my recommendation that readers scrutinize potentially misleading information on subjects such as taxes.

In closing, my hope is that you find the information in this book not only an educational eye-opener, but useful in your quest to legitimately reduce your tax liabilities while avoiding the IRS radar.

GLOSSARY

Adjusted Gross Income

A taxpayer's gross income minus certain adjustments. The IRS uses the AGI to determine how much income tax a taxpayer may owe.

Annual Gift Exclusion

An annual exclusion gift is a **gift that can be included in the donor's yearly exclusion**. The annual exclusion is a tax benefit that taxpayers can use when giving a gift that exceeds the exclusion amount.

Capital Gains

A profit from the sale of property or an investment.

Charitable Donations

Donations of money or other assets given, without restrictions or obligations to 501 (c) (3) public or private recognized charities.

Civil Service System

A system of legislation established dictating who may delegate to a board of civil service commissioners the authority to make rules consistent with existing laws, to conduct investigations, and generally to exercise any and all administrative measures necessary and proper to achieve the objectives and purposes of the civil service laws.

Cost Basis

The **original cost of property**, adjusted for factors such as depreciation. When property is sold, the taxpayer pays/ (saves) taxes on a capital gain / (loss) that equals the amount realized on the sale minus the sold property's basis.

Deduction Allowances

Allowable Deductions are the **deductions allowed by IRS to a taxpayer to be subtracted from their gross income for a particular taxable year.**

Dependents

A **person who relies on someone else for financial support and can include children or other relatives**. Having a dependent can entitle a taxpayer to claim a dependency exemption on their tax return. A taxpayer who can demonstrate that they have a dependent also may be able to use this filing status to qualify for certain tax credits.

Depreciation

The process of recovering the cost spent on an asset over time, to acquire an asset until it is recovered.

Discriminant Index Function System Scoring

A system that rates the potential for change, based on past IRS experience with similar returns. The Unreported Income DIF (UIDIF) score rates the return for the potential of unreported income.

Fiduciary Plan Administrator

A person that has a duty to act in the interest of the plan's participants or employees, not the company that employs them.

Fraudulent Tax Credit

Person files a tax return and knowingly commits a **fraudulent** activity by claiming of a **tax credit** by him or any other person.

Fraudulent Tax Return

A tax return in which an individual attempt to file using someone else's name or Social Security Number (<u>SSN</u>) on the return or where the tax-payer is presenting documents or information that have no basis.

Grey Tax Law Areas

A position taken not clear in law whether it is acceptable or unacceptable is determinable by interpretation.

Gross Earnings

Refers to the **total earnings of an individual**, prior to deductions for income taxes and other taxes, as well as any deductions imposed by the employer.

Information Returns Processing System

System that **receives data submitted by employers and other third parties (payers) reporting taxpayer income such as wages, pensions, interest and dividends paid during the tax year**. This information is validated and stored in the Information Return Master File (IRMF). IRP also has two Correlation projects which attempts to match income reported on information returns against income reported by taxpayers on their individual income tax returns.

Itemized Deductions

Expenses that can be subtracted from adjusted gross income (AGI) to reduce your tax bill. Itemized deductions must be listed on <u>Schedule A</u> of

Form 1040. 1 Most taxpayers have the option to either itemize deductions or claim the standard deduction that applies to their filing status.

Joint Resolution

A **legislative measure**, which requires the approval of both chambers and, with one exception (i.e., proposal to amend the U.S. Constitution), is submitted just as a bill to the president for signature in to law. Joint resolutions considered to have the same effect as a bill.

Like-Kind of Exchange

A like-kind exchange is a **tax-deferred transaction** that allows for the disposal of an asset and the acquisition of another similar asset without generating a capital gains tax liability from the sale of the first asset.

Net Corporate Income

The amount of accounting profit a corporation has left over after paying off all its expenses.

Non-Employee Compensation

Money you earn as a contractor, consultant, freelancer, or other independent worker. It's legally supposed to be reported on 1099-MISC (Box 7), 1099-K (Box 1a), or as cash, check or credit card sales transactions. Requires you to complete Schedule C. You can deduct expense related to the income.

Offer In Compromise

Revenue Service that settles a taxpayer's tax liabilities for less than the full amount owed. Taxpayers who can fully pay the liabilities through an installment agreement or other means, generally won't qualify for an OIC in most cases.

Ordinary Income

Ordinary income, income earned or income profit from the sale of property or investment assets, is the **money you receive from an activity**. Ordinary Income is subject to ordinary, or marginal, income tax rates outlined by the IRS.

Patronage System

A system of **personal ties and networks in which a patron or superior offered protection and support to an inferior or client, who owed him loyalty and service in return.**

Personal Exemptions

An **amount that a resident taxpayer is entitled to claim as a tax deduction against personal income in calculating taxable income and consequently federal income tax.**

Progressive Tax Rate

A progressive tax is based on the taxpayer's ability to pay. It imposes a lower tax rate on low-income earners than on those with a higher income. This is usually achieved by creating tax brackets that group taxpayers by income ranges.

Prohibition

The action of forbidding something, especially by law. The Prohibition in the United States was the action taken by the government forbidding the sale, use, and transfer of alcohol beverages.

Self-Employed Earnings

Refers to a person who operates a business or profession as a sole proprietor, partner in a partnership, independent contractor, or consultant.

Self-employed individuals report their income on Schedule C of Form 1040. Self-employment typically involves bearing the expenses of hiring others to assist or do work on one's own behalf, having to personally bear the risk of success or failure of the business, and bearing responsibility for correcting unsatisfactory work.

Statute of Collection Is Tolled

The judgment creditor (party to whom judgment is owed-The IRS) will have extra time to enforce or collect on the debt.

Substitute for Return

The IRS prepares the return solely based on information it has from your employers, banks, and other payers. An SFR has a filing status of single or married filing separately.

Tariffs

A tax or duty to be paid on a particular class of imports or exports.

Tax Audit

IRS thoroughly double checks a person or corporation's tax filings. Audits generally happen on the last three years of tax returns but can go back as far as six years. Many factors can increase a person's likelihood of being audited, from high income to rounded, estimated numbers on tax forms.

Tax Deficiency

An assessment of Taxes, as a result of a Final Determination, an unpaid tax liability, or a similar nature causing a taxpayer to owe more taxes than paid.

Tax Enforcement Compliance

Taxpayers' – whether individuals or businesses – decisions to comply with state, federal, and international tax laws and regulations in a timely manner.

Tax Lien

A tax lien is a **lien imposed by law upon a property to secure the payment of taxes**. A tax lien may be imposed for delinquent taxes owed on real property or personal property, or as a result of failure to pay income taxes or other taxes.

Unreported Income Function Scoring System

A system that rates the tax return for the potential of unreported income.

The Revolutionary War to the War of 1812. (n.d.). The Tax Analyst. Retrieved May 14, 2022, from http://taxhistory.tax.org/www/website.nsf/Web/THM1777?OpenDocument.

continental congress. (2010, February 4). History.Com Editors. Retrieved May 14, 2022, from https://www.history.com/topics/american-revolution/the-continental-congress.

History, Art & Archives, U.S. House of Representatives, "Power of the Purse," https://history.house.gov/Institution/Origins-Development/Power-of-the-Purse/ (June 19, 2022).

History of the Treasury. (n.d.). Https://Home.Treasury.Gov/about/History/History-Overview/History-of-the-Treasury. Retrieved March 28, 2022, from https://home.treasury.gov/about/history/history-overview/history-of-the-treasury.

F.N.A. (2011). The Regional Newsletter of The Friends of the National Archives and The National Archives at Atlanta. *THE CIVIL HISTORY.* Retrieved July 4, 2022 from https://archives.gov/file/atlanta/newletter/2011-july.pdf 2011-july.pdf (archives.gov).

Fox, Cynthia G. "Income Tax Records of the Civil War Years." *Https://Www.Archives.Gov/Publications/Prologue/1986/Winter/Civil-War-Tax-Records.Html,* National Archives, 1986, www.archives.gov/publications/prologue/1986/winter/civil-war-tax-records.html.

Magness, P. W. (2019, February 14). *The Real History of Us Income Tax.* Https://Www.Aier.Org/Article/the-Real-History-of-the-American-Income-Tax/. Retrieved May 1, 2022, from https://www.aier.org/article/the-real-history-of-the-american-income-tax/.

"IRS History Timeline." *Https://Www.Irs.Gov/Irs-History-Timeline,* https://www.irs.gov/irs-history-timeline, www.irs.gov/irs-history-timeline. Accessed 16 May 2022.

Fontinelle, Amy. "A Brief History of Taxes in the U.S." *Https://Www.Investopedia.Com/Articles/Tax/10/History-Taxes.Asp,* Investopia, 22 Mar. 2022, www.investopedia.com/articles/tax/10/history-taxes.asp.

"The Financial Crisis of the 1870s" *World History,* 6 Aug. 2017, https://www.worldhistory.us/american-history/the-financial-crisis-of-the-1870s.php. Accessed 28 July 2022.

"The White House Historical Association. Building The Whitehouse." https://
www.whitehousehistory.org/, www.whitehousehistory.org. Accessed 17
May 2022.

US General Services Administration. https://www.gsa.gov/real-estate/histor-
ic-preservation/explore-historic-buildings/find-a-build-search. Date Retrieved
01 June 2022 14:27.

Find a Building: Search. (n.d.). Https://Www.Gsa.Gov/Real-Estate/Historic-
Preservation/Explore-Historic-Buildings/Find-a-Building-Search. Retrieved June
1, 2022, from https://www.gsa.gov/real-estate/historic-preservation/explore-his-
toric-buildings/find-a-building-search.

"Congress.Gov." *Congress.Gov*, Congress.gov, www.congress.gov/
search?q=%7B%22congress%22%3A%22all%22%2C%-
22source%22%3A%22all%22%2C%22search%22%3A%22offer+in+compro-
mise%22%7D&pageSort=dateOfIntroduction%3Aasc&pageSize=100&page=4.
Accessed 20 June 2022.

"16th Amendment to the U.S. Constitution: Federal Income Tax (1913)." *Https://
Www.Archives.Gov/Publications/Prologue/1986/Winter/Civil-War-Tax-Records.
Html*, National Archives, www.archives.gov/publications/prologue/1986/winter/
civil-war-tax-records.html. Accessed 22 Nov. 2021.

The Marshall Plan. Hoover Digest. Hoover Institute: By Peter J. Duignan and
Lewis H. Gann, Thursday, October 30, 1997. https://www.hoover.org/research/
marshal-plan. text. Date Retrieved 01 June 2022 15:34.

"Financing, World War I." Americans at War. . *Encyclopedia.com*. 21 Jun.
2022 <https://www.encyclopedia.com>. Date retrieved 13 July 2022 12:44.

Social Security History. (n.d.). The Social Security Administration. Retrieved May
29, 2022, from https://www.ssa.gov/history/orghist.html.

Historical Background And Development Of Social Security. (n.d.). Https://Www.
Ssa.Gov/History/Briefhistory3.Html. Retrieved May 29, 2022, from https://www.
ssa.gov/history/briefhistory3.html.

The Social Security Act. (n.d.). Https://Www.Hhttps://Www.History.Com/Topics/
Great-Depression/Social-Security-Actistory.Com/Topics/Great-Depression/
Social-Security-Act. Retrieved July 30, 2022, from https://www.history.com/
topics/great-depression/social-security-act.

Social Security & Medicare Tax Rates. (n.d.). Https://Www.Ssa.Gov/OACT/ProgData/taxRates.Html. Retrieved June 1, 2022, from https://www.ssa.gov/OACT/ProgData/taxRates.html.

Information Returns Processing. (n.d.). Https://Www.Irs.Gov/Privacy-Disclosure/Information-Returns-Processing. Retrieved May 13, 2022, from https://www.irs.gov/privacy-disclosure/information-returns-processing.

Internal Revenue Service. (2001, August). Https://www.*PREDICTORS OF UNREPORTED INCOME: TEST OF UNREPORTED INCOME (UI) DIF SCORES* (Prepared for the Internal Revenue Service Research Conference, June 11–12, 2002). Dennis Cyr, Internal Revenue Service.

"2017 IRS Nationwide Tax Forum Tax Audits: Triggers and Tips Are You Really Going to File That Return? An Audit Target!!" *2017 IRS Nationwide Tax Forum*, 2017, Retrieved from www.irs.gov/pub/irs-utl/2017ntf-irsauditstriggers.pdf.

"Here's What Taxpayers Need to Know about Paying Taxes on Their Hobby Activities." www.irs.gov/newsroom/heres-what-taxpayers-need-to-know-about-paying-taxes-on-their-hobby-activities. Accessed 13 May 2022.

Thomas Eckhardt, Internal Revenue Service Lou Ann Sandoval, Internal Revenue Service Marvin Halldorson Denver field office of Small Business/Self-Employed Research. Web. 13 2022. Retrieved from https://www.irs.gov/pub/irs-soi/puidif2.pdf.

About Publication 556, Examination of Returns, Appeal Rights, and Claims for Refund. (n.d.). Https://Www.Irs.Gov/Forms-Pubs/about-Publication-556. Retrieved May 13, 2022, from https://www.irs.gov/forms-pubs/about-publication-556.

[1] *Orlando sisters sentenced in $25 million tax fraud scheme. Internal Revenue Service.* (2021, August 17). Retrieved May 14, 2022, from https://www.irs.gov/compliance/criminal-investigation/orlando-sisters-sentenced-in-25-million-tax-fraud-scheme.

How small business owners can deduct their home office from their taxes. (2022, January 19). Irs.Gov. Retrieved April 10, 2022, from https://www.irs.gov/newsroom/how-small-business-owners-can-deduct-their-home-office-from-their-taxes.

Topic No. 511 Business Travel Expenses. (n.d.). Https://Www.Irs.Gov/Taxtopics/Tc511. Retrieved May 24, 2022, from https://www.irs.gov/taxtopics/tc511.

Publication 523 (2021), Selling Your Home. (n.d.). Https://Www.Irs.Gov/ Publications/P523. Retrieved May 13, 2022, from https://www.irs.gov/publications/p523.

Publication 527, Residential Rental Property. (n.d.). Https://Www.Irs.Gov/ Forms-Pubs/about-Publication-527. Retrieved May 13, 2022, from https://www.irs.gov/publications/p527.

Publication 501 (2021), Dependents, Standard Deduction, and Filing Information. (n.d.). Https://Www.Irs.Gov/Publications/P501. Retrieved May 13, 2022, from https://www.irs.gov/publications/p501.

Publication 526 (2021), Charitable Contributions. (n.d.). Https://Www.Irs.Gov/ Publications/P526. Retrieved May 13, 2022, from https://www.irs.gov/publications/p526.

Instructions for Form 709 (2021) United States Gift (and Generation-Skipping Transfer) Tax Return. (n.d.). Https://Www.Irs.Gov/Instructions/I709. Retrieved May 13, 2022, from https://www.irs.gov/instructions/i709.

Free File Alliance. Wikipedia contributors, *Wikipedia, The Free Encyclopedia.* Date of last revision: 14 January 2022 17:25 UTC, Date retrieved: 25 February 2022 21:44 UTC, Permanent link: https://en.wikipedia.org/w/index. php?title=Free_File_Alliance&oldid=1065659792

Primary contributors: revision history statistics, Page Version ID: 1065659792.

Free File do your federal tax for free Free File. (n.d.). Https://Www.Irs.Gov/Filing/ Free-File-Do-Your-Federal-Taxes-for-Free. Retrieved May 24, 2022, from https://www.irs.gov/filing/free-file-do-your-federal-taxes-for-free.

I.R.C. Sections 61(a), 62, 102(a), 121(a), 121(b)(2), 121(b)(3), 152(a), 152(c)(1), 152(d)(1), 152(d)(2), 152(d)(3), 162, 162(a)(2), 170(a)(1), 170(b), 170(b)(1)(A), 170(b)(1)(G), 170(b)(1)(B), 179, 280(a), 280(c)(1), 280(c)(1)(A), 280A(d)(2), 280A(d)(3), 280A(f)(1), 501(c)(3), 501(c)(7), 691(a)(1), 1031, 1231, 1245, 2512(b), 2503(c)(1), 6012(1)(A), 6501(a), 6501(b)(1), 6501(c), 6511(a), 6511(a)(1), 7201, 7602, 7605, 7206(1), 7206(2), 7606(2).